WHEN GOOD PEOPLE WRITE *BAD* SENTENCES

WHEN GOOD PEOPLE WRITE BAD SENTENCES

12 Steps to
Better Writing Habits

Robert W. Harris

 ST. MARTIN'S GRIFFIN ✖ NEW YORK

www.stmartins.com

Library of Congress Cataloging-in-Publication Data

Harris, Robert W., 1954–
    When good people write bad sentences : 12 steps to better writing habits / Robert W. Harris.
            p. cm.
    ISBN 0-312-32804-4
    1. English language—Usage—Handbooks, manuals, etc. 2. English language—Grammar—Handbooks, manuals, etc. 3. English language—Rhetoric—Handbooks, manuals, etc. I. Title.
    PE1460.H3878   2004
    808'.042—dc22

                                                              2003026326

First Edition: June 2004

10 9 8 7 6 5 4 3 2 1

CONTENTS

ACKNOWLEDGMENTS

I would like to thank everyone at St. Martin's Press who helped make this book a reality. Special thanks go to my editor, Marian Lizzi, for her constructive criticism and attention to detail. Thanks go also to Liz and Buster for their support and inspiration.

THE TWELVE STEPS TO
VERBAL ENLIGHTENMENT

1. Accept the fact that bad writing happens.
2. Admit you've willingly made writing mistakes.
3. Believe that Standard English can heal you.
4. Stop writing weak sentences.
5. Stop writing formal sentences.
6. Stop writing overweight sentences.
7. Stop writing unclear sentences.
8. Stop writing careless sentences.
9. Stop writing unpersuasive sentences.
10. Stop writing incongruous sentences.
11. Stop writing unstructured sentences.
12. Stop writing unsightly sentences.

WHEN GOOD PEOPLE WRITE BAD SENTENCES

INTRODUCTION

IN 1986 ADAM W. DANGLED HIS FIRST PARTICIPLE. And he liked it. He liked it a lot. Thus began ten years of dependence on nonstandard grammar, questionable syntax, and careless punctuation. Adam was living on the edge of miscommunication. And he was hurting the very ones who wanted to understand his prose.

But you wouldn't know any of that if you met Adam today. He's a successful businessman, loving husband, and proud father. What turned his life around? He stopped abusing the English language. In fact he can tell you the exact date of his last run-on sentence: September 14, 1996. It was then that he encountered the power of Standard English. And ever since that day, his writing has been clear, concise, and confident.

Perhaps there's a little Adam W. in all of us. At one

time or another, each of us has been tempted to forget the rules and the commonsense guidelines. Some can resist, but many are drawn slowly into the abyss of bad writing habits. As they relax their standards, they become addicted to weak, sloppy, unclear, poorly planned communication. And it's not just the victim who gets hurt. When one of us writes poorly, we all suffer.

It Can't Happen to Me

ADAM ALWAYS HAD THOUGHT THAT BAD WRITING was something that befell other people. He was wrong. "It can't happen to me" is an all-too-familiar refrain, but it doesn't change reality. Almost anyone can get caught in the iron grip of lackadaisical grammar, punctuation, and style. (I, personally, never have had such a problem.) They might easily recognize someone else's bad writing, but when it comes to their own writing skills, they are in denial.

Bad writers often believe that they are doing a good job of hiding their problem. But every time they put words on paper, they leave telltale signs: a missing comma, a plural pronoun referring to a singular noun, a timeworn phrase. Like most people, I found bad writing annoying and frustrating, but I pretended not to notice. Then one day I came across this item in an office newsletter:

We have not taken our current can alotment to be turned in and we have quite a lot of them. With the current addition that should bring us up monetarily further than we have been.

At that moment my frustration turned to compassion. I realized that something had to be done. Bad writers obviously couldn't help themselves, so I decided to help. I realized the urgent need to loosen the shackles of uncertain style and usage. I wanted people to know that they could overcome their addiction, embrace Standard English, and restore their desire to write well. So I committed myself to finding a way to help bad writing addicts understand their affliction and attain some level of verbal enlightenment.

The Program

THE FRUIT OF MY LABOR IS A SIMPLE BUT POWERFUL twelve-step program for recovering from addiction to bad writing. As with so many addictions, bad writing can develop gradually over a period of years. And the victim is often unaware of even having a problem. So this book challenges readers to take an objective look at themselves and their writing and find the courage to begin the process of change.

My program treats the tendency toward bad writing as

a universal human condition. In some people, it lies dormant; in others, it creates mild problems; and in others, it manifests itself as *malescribism*, an uncontrollable urge to write carelessly and unpersuasively. So the 12 steps don't provide solutions to isolated problems in the neatly segregated categories of punctuation, syntax, diction, and style. Instead, the steps help malescribes understand the emotional foundations and psychological forces behind those problems. Only with this deep understanding can permanent changes take place.

The heart of this approach is a focus on the *functional* unit of writing: the sentence. We'll look at nine types of ineffective sentences that arise from a swirling brew of unexamined emotions, attitudes, and beliefs. This complex, integrated approach will help malescribes learn to take a broader and healthier perspective. They can then aim for the general goals of clarity, conciseness, correctness, and persuasiveness in their writing.

How the Book Is Organized

WHEN GOOD PEOPLE WRITE BAD SENTENCES PRESents strategies for overcoming self-destructive needs that are satisfied by bad writing habits. In each step you'll learn about the emotional bases for mistakes and misjudgments in writing.

The first three steps will help you overcome the need for **resistance.** Here you will be led gently into the process of self-examination and healing. As you'll find out, it's possible to hate the writing but love the writer. Here we'll look at:

- *Denial,* which makes it difficult for one to accept the fact that bad writing exists and that its lure is powerful.
- *Pride,* which manifests itself in an unwillingness to take responsibility for one's own writing problems.
- *Suspicion,* which prevents one from embracing the twelve-step program and accepting the healing power of Standard English.

In steps 4, 5, and 6, you'll find help in conquering the need for **approval.** You will be challenged to begin moving toward independence of thought and confidence in action. You will be encouraged to change, keeping in mind that change is an ongoing process. Here, the focus will be on:

- *Insecurity,* which manifests itself in weak, passive, and qualified sentences.
- *Worry,* which is evident whenever one writes formal, flowery, or pretentious sentences.

- *Shame,* which manifests itself in overweight sentences, needless repetition, and digressions.

Steps 7, 8, and 9 will help you overcome the need for **control.** In these steps, you will be weaned gradually from the emotional comfort of common bad writing habits. You'll find that you have wings and that flight is possible. Here we'll examine:

- *Indifference,* which is behind unclear sentences containing jargon, abbreviations, and vague references.
- *Regret,* which creates the conditions for careless sentences.
- *Doubt,* which is the basis for unpersuasive sentences lacking clear expectations or motivation for readers.

And in the final three steps, you'll find assistance in overcoming the need for **defiance.** In these three steps, you'll be encouraged to confront any remaining unresolved family issues. This psychological purging is the final phase in the healing process. Here you can learn to defeat:

- *Anger,* which is the basis for dissonant and incongruous sentences.

- *Rebelliousness,* which leads to unstructured sentences that ignore readers' perceptual and attention limitations.
- *Stubbornness,* which is evident in unsightly sentences presented in inappropriate fonts and carelessly formatted pages.

Throughout the 12 steps, you'll find many "healing tips" to help speed your recovery. And at the end of the road, you'll find a final word of encouragement and the "Recovering Malescribe's Bill of Rights."

The Power to Change

WHEN GOOD PEOPLE WRITE BAD SENTENCES IS THE first book to face reality and treat bad writing as what it is: an addiction. Once you accept this fact, the healing can begin. It's a long and rocky road, and not everyone starts at the same place. But the goal for each of us is the same: overcoming dependence on questionable grammar, syntax, and style.

You are not helpless. You can attain verbal enlightenment. You can start today simply by taking the first step. If you don't, you could be on the path to ruin and despair. The choice is yours.

ACCEPT THE FACT THAT
BAD WRITING HAPPENS

(by Overcoming Denial)

JANET H., FRED S., AND PAT C.* ARE THREE HAPPY individuals. Janet's a nuclear engineer who enjoys Scrabble, Italian cooking, and walks on the beach. Fred teaches high school history and spends his spare time restoring an old Chevy pickup and watching C-SPAN. And Pat's a twenty-something executive assistant with a desire to travel and a knack for origami. They're just three hard-working people with different backgrounds and different interests. But until recently they had something in common: they all suffered from *malescribism*, an uncontrollable urge to write badly. It was apparent to everyone around them, but they didn't have a clue.

*Their real names.

Janet Expected Others
to Be Good Readers

"OH, I MIGHT OMIT A COMMA NOW AND THEN," Janet often would say. "But it's not a *problem*." Janet was a nice person and a valued employee, but her writing was sloppy. As with most intuitive punctuators, she was well-intentioned in her writing but careless with the details. "They'll know what I mean," she said whenever someone would point out a missing comma or misplaced apostrophe.

But her readers *didn't* always know what she meant. By relying on her own quirky punctuation guidelines, Janet was unwittingly confusing her readers. It was often a challenge to figure out what she was trying to say. Said one coworker, "When it came from Janet, you just *knew* you would be doing a lot of rereading to understand what she meant."

Janet felt that good reading could make up for bad writing. But was it really fair to expect others to clean up her mess?

Fred Tried to Fit In

"LOOK, I'M JUST A *SOCIAL* MISSPELLER." THAT'S WHAT Fred had to say when asked if he might need to pay a little more attention to his writing. His attitude was that if everyone spells poorly, why worry about it? He didn't want to be seen as an intellectual snob or a stickler for details. As with all rule-bending justifiers, Fred tried to hide among other offenders.

"I'm no different from anyone else," he would say. He would even make jokes to avoid dealing directly with his problem. "If I don't know how to spell a word, how can I look it up?" he often would quip. Fred's colleagues would just shake their heads in frustration.

Fred thought "close is good enough" was the best guideline when it came to spelling. But is it?

Pat Felt Restricted by Rules

"HEY, THE SYNTAX I USE IS MY *OWN* D—— BUSIness!" That was Pat's response whenever anyone would question her arrangement of words. To her, writing was all about feelings and individuality. "I'm trying to communicate in my own voice, not please a bunch of picky readers," she would explain impatiently.

Pat was convinced that the accepted rules of writing were designed solely to stifle her creativity. But by exercising her "freedom" of expression, she was creating problems for others. Like most syntax abusers, she continually confused and frustrated her readers. And the impact was felt at home as well. "It wasn't so bad when we got married," said her husband, "but it seemed to get worse as time went by."

Pat thought that her readers would be so involved with her ideas that they would overlook the way she arranged words. But would they?

AS YOU CAN SEE, ADDICTION TO BAD WRITING CAN manifest itself in many ways. It can cloud judgment. It can hurt relationships. It can lead to anxiety, guilt, self-loathing, and, yes, even malaise. And the central theme is always *denial*. Oh, our three friends saw the problem in others but not in themselves. They convinced themselves there was no cause for concern. They couldn't see the damage their writing was doing. And the worse their writing got, the better their rationalizations became.

Fortunately, Janet, Fred, and Pat are now in recovery. As survivors of malescribism, they now see each day as an opportunity to write clear, correct, well-organized prose. How did they do it? How did they pull themselves up from the depths of verbal suffering and despair? They did it by admitting that they had a problem and that the problem had become unmanageable by their own efforts. With determination, they each learned and embraced Standard English, followed the twelve-step recovery program, and ultimately regained control of their lives.

What about *you*, friend? Do you think that you, or someone you know, might suffer from malescribism? Do you know enough about the disorder to come to an informed decision? You've probably got lots of questions, so let's learn a little more about this all-too-common affliction.

Understanding the Problem

"What is malescribism"?[*1]

MALESCRIBISM IS THE TENDENCY TO WRITE BADLY. It is a set of dysfunctional responses to the demands of communicating in print. Instead of carefully and thoughtfully conveying a clear, confident message, malescribes string words together in an intuitive way, disregarding many of the accepted conventions of grammar, syntax, and style.

In the past, we thought that bad writing was simply the result of making individual mistakes, such as mis-

---

* Note: The questions that introduce topics in this book (except in step 12) contain grammatical or stylistic mistakes. See how many you can spot (it's fun!). The mistakes are explained at the end of each chapter.

spelling a word or dangling a participle. Malescribes were seen as "weak" or lacking in willpower. They simply weren't trying hard enough.

But today, we have a better understanding of the problem. We now know that the tendency to write badly is a human condition, and its seed is in all of us. Individual sins of omission (such as leaving out a needed comma) or commission (such as pointless redundancy) are merely reflections of that condition. For some people the disorder is mild, creating only minor communication problems. But for others it can be a life-draining malady.

The Roots of Bad Writing

"Why does bad-writing happen?"[2]

BAD WRITING HAS TO HAVE A CAUSE. IS IT POOR teaching? Dysfunctional family experiences? Unresolved psychosexual tensions? Or is it genetic? Sure, it's all of these, and we'll explore the roots of malescribism in detail during the course of the twelve steps. Regardless of the cause, the effects of the affliction can be devastating: lives in chaos, families torn apart, careers ruined.

The Victims of Malescribism

"I'm a college graduate, go to church, and am a registered Republican—so I probably have nothing to worry about, writingwise, I mean."[3]

IF YOU THINK YOUR STATION IN LIFE PROTECTS YOU from malescribism, think again. This malady is no respecter of status, nor does it take into account social, ethnic, or religious orientation. Malescribes are black and white, male and female, believer and nonbeliever, liberal and conservative. Malescribism is the great equalizer.

You must understand that addiction to bad writing has nothing to do with habits or beliefs. And sufferers aren't being punished by God—that's reserved for red-light runners and doctors who keep people waiting. Malescribes are distinguished from good writers only by the quality of their writing. It's important to separate the writer from the writing.

The Progressive Nature of Malescribism

"What coarse does malescribism follow? Will it go away on its own by itself?"[4]

MALESCRIBISM IS A PROGRESSIVE DISORDER: IT GETS worse over time. And it won't go away by itself because it's a self-maintaining process. Malescribes write poorly to enter an emotional comfort zone. Later they deny the problem, blame others, and make excuses. These behaviors lead to anxiety and the need for more emotional comfort, and so they return to their friend, the poorly constructed sentence. It is a vicious cycle.

This Book Can Help

IN THIS BOOK, MY GOAL IS TO HELP PEOPLE UNDERstand the roots of bad writing. Once the psychological bases for writing problems and misjudgments become clear, the healing process can begin. To facilitate change, I offer a twelve-step program for recovery. But unlike other such programs, mine doesn't require that you come to grips with your character defects. What you do in private is none of my business. Here we're going to focus on diction, grammar, and style.

Embracing Step 1

"I'm not sure if I suffer from malescribism: but, I do want to learn more about it. Should I follow the twelve steps?"[5]

REGARDLESS OF YOUR PERSONAL SITUATION, YOU can and should at least take the first step. All are welcome on the road to recovery. So let's begin together. The first step toward recovery will free you from the need to deny the existence of malescribism.

Step 1: Accept the fact that bad writing happens.

Understand that it doesn't happen just to "them." No, malescribism affects people from all walks of life. It can strike anyone—even decent, well-intentioned people like you and me. The first step is admitting the problem.

Endnotes

1. The closing quotation mark should go outside the question mark.
2. No hyphen is needed in the phrase "bad writing."
3. "Go to church" should be "a churchgoer." "Writingwise" is clumsy.
4. "Coarse" should be "course." "On its own by itself" is redundant.
5. The colon should be a comma. No comma is needed after "but."

ADMIT YOU'VE WILLINGLY MADE WRITING MISTAKES

(by Overcoming Pride)

BEFORE THEY GET HELP, ALMOST ALL MALESCRIBES allow *pride* to block the road to recovery. For many, it's a well-honed defense against admitting any shortcoming or difficulty in writing. For others, it's a spontaneous reaction to a perceived threat to their self-esteem. But for all sufferers, it stands in the way of healthy writing.

Pride can take a variety of forms, each of which helps malescribes convince themselves that the problem is "out there." Perhaps it's the fault of their readers. Or maybe the educational system is to blame. Or maybe society's expectations are unrealistic. The list is long.

Rationalization

LET'S START WITH *RATIONALIZATION*, A DEFENSIVE technique that helps us turn our liabilities into assets, make bad habits seem good, and avoid dealing with problems altogether. Most of us have considerable skill in using it.

"Just because I use extra, unnecessary, redundant words doesn't mean I'm writing poorly. I'm just trying to clearly elucidate my printed message."[1]

MALESCRIBES OFTEN DEFEND WORDINESS AS A NEC-essary part of writing clearly and creatively. But in reality, superfluous words dilute the impact of a sentence and add nothing to its meaning. For example, writing *in order to* instead of the succinct *to* suggests that some padding was needed to give the sentence an acceptable length. So wordiness can actually suggest that you have *little* to say.

"Sometimes, my coworkers complain about my use of all uppercase letters in my e-mails. BUT I'M JUST TRYING TO GET THEIR ATTENTION."[2]

PRIDE CAN LEAD TO THE USE OF UNCONVENTIONAL text formatting. This technique is used in an effort to at-

---

tract attention or convey seriousness or authority and thereby satisfy the writer's ego. But it comes across as shouting, and many people won't even bother to read it. Furthermore, it makes it difficult to see which parts of the message are most important. So unusual text formatting will often repel rather than attract.

Indifference

"I've never been too concerned about commas, apostrophes and dashes—they're just not that important."[3]

IMAGINE A PROFESSIONAL PHOTOGRAPHER SAYING, "I've never been too concerned about my camera battery. It's small—it's just not that important." Ridiculous. We all know that the value of a battery has nothing to do with its size.

But when putting words on paper, malescribes become unconcerned about the small, yet crucial, elements of punctuation. They let pride keep them from attending to the "lowly" comma, apostrophe, and dash. They feel that because these items are small, they must be relatively unimportant. But if readers become confused, then the smallest item has, in fact, become the largest, hasn't it?

The Problem with Pride

THE BEST WAY TO UNDERSTAND PRIDE IS TO REALIZE its irony. Malescribes firmly believe that their writing achieves one effect, when in reality it usually has the *opposite* effect. Wordiness suggests that you have little to say. Unusual text formatting draws attention to itself and away from the message. Indifference to small punctuation marks makes an impact.

Pride blinds us to the fact that we're not achieving our goals. It creates a filter that reinterprets reality. And through that filter, we come to see our poorly conceived and sloppily executed prose as adequate, well-intentioned, or even creative. Thus writing becomes a self-defeating process. The harder we try, the less effective our writing becomes. Pride prevents us from owning up to the problem.

Embracing Step 2

NOW THAT YOU UNDERSTAND THE WAYS THAT PRIDE may have obscured your questionable writing habits, you're ready to move ahead. You're ready to understand *your* role in *your* problem. The second step toward recovery will free you from the need to use pride to protect yourself from the truth about your bad writing habits.

Step 2: Admit you've willingly made writing mistakes.

It's the "willingly" part that creates the power in this crucial step. When you begin to work through this step, it means that you've finally decided to take responsibility for your writing problems. You are beginning to empower yourself.

But how bad is the problem? To what extent has male-scribism taken control of your life? Let's try to find out.

Questions to Consider

TO HELP YOU DETERMINE THE IMPACT OF MALE-scribism in your life, I've put together a list of ten questions. They aren't meant to be judgmental, but are provided to open the door of understanding. So give each one careful consideration.

1. Have you ever felt you should cut back on slang and colloquialisms?
2. Do you get a lift by splitting an infinitive or dangling a participle?
3. Have you ever awoken in the morning with no memory of your stylistic mistakes of the day before?

4. Do you sometimes mix metaphors to steady your nerves?
5. Have you ever argued with family members about your grammar?
6. Have you ever stopped misspelling, only to resume your old habits a few days later?
7. Has your punctuation ever caused difficulties at work or at home?
8. Do the phrases "past history," "advance warning," and "very unique" look all right to you?
9. Does your wordiness increase around the holidays?
10. Does indifference to syntax make you feel special?

If you're waiting for a scoring system, you're out of luck. There's no scoring on this quiz. A number can't tell you where you are in your struggle with malescribism. Only you can decide.

Endnotes

1. Both sentences are too wordy.
2. Using all uppercase letters makes a sentence hard to read.
3. A comma should come after "apostrophes." The apostrophe is missing from "theyre."

BELIEVE THAT STANDARD ENGLISH CAN HEAL YOU

(by Overcoming Suspicion)

IN WORKING THROUGH STEP 2, YOU ADMITTED THAT you willingly had made writing errors. But will you continue to make them? The grip of malescribism is strong—too strong for most sufferers to overcome without help. So if you plan to take back your life and begin to write well again, you're going to need to admit the truth: your writing problem has become unmanageable. You've tried, exerted your willpower, and made promises to yourself. Yet you're still addicted to bad writing.

People who are in recovery from malescribism at some point came to understand that they couldn't do it on their own. They accepted the fact that they didn't have the power to overcome their addiction to bad writing. They eventually had to take a leap of faith and look to something bigger and more powerful for assistance.

A Greater Power

MALESCRIBES IN RECOVERY ALL CAME TO UNDERstand they needed help. They realized, reluctantly, that there was no shame in seeking guidance. And they eventually accepted the fact that there was a power greater than any individual writer. We call it Standard English.

Exactly what is Standard English? It's a collection of accepted guidelines for communicating effectively in print. Whereas malescribes wonder about what is correct, people who trust in Standard English know confidently that they are writing in a way that people will understand. It replaces guessing with order and certainty. It takes a burden off our shoulders, freeing us to focus on developing our ideas.

Despite the advantages of relying on Standard English, many malescribes have trouble trusting in this higher power. They are, in a word, *suspicious*. And their suspicion slows their progress toward recovery.

How Suspicion Works

SUSPICION IS A PSYCHOLOGICAL MECHANISM THAT protects us from real or imagined threats. When properly channeled, it can save us embarrassment, heartache, or pain. But improperly channeled, suspicion can prevent us from seeing and taking advantage of opportunities. It can magnify potential problems and obscure potential payoffs.

Malescribes often take suspicion to unhealthy levels. So let's look at how suspicion can work to keep people from embracing Standard English and starting on the road to recovery.

Confrontation

WHEN WE ENCOUNTER SOMETHING NEW THAT IS highly touted by others, we sometimes express our suspicions through *confrontation*. We vigorously challenge the proposed ideas and the sincerity of the people who believe in them. We are, in a sense, reverting to an instinctual response.

"Who's ideas are these? Who put you in charge?"[1]

NO ONE CAN TELL YOU HOW TO WRITE. WE WHO have traveled the path to verbal enlightenment merely want to explain the benefits of relying on a higher power. The decision to trust in Standard English must be a personal one based on rational consideration of the facts and the potential benefits.

"Who made these writing __rules__? Some egghead in an ivory tower??"[2]

IT'S A MISTAKE TO THINK THAT PROPER ENGLISH WAS created by pedantic individuals removed from the real world. In fact, the fundamentals of clear writing developed slowly over centuries. Practical usage and thoughtful evaluation by people from all walks of life created Standard English. Today we have a time-tested system that ensures effective written communication. And contrary to what some might suspect, it does not inhibit fresh or effective expression.

Confrontation is usually a knee-jerk reaction. Despite the desire to improve, malescribes initially take an aggressive stance that inhibits progress. But learning some facts about Standard English is usually enough to interrupt this unproductive thought process. Once addicts understand the origins and purpose of Standard English, they become able at least to admit the *possibility* that it has power.

The Need for Control

"I dont want to be seen as weak willed, I'm pretty sure I can overcome malescribism on my own. After all, I am a college graduate."[3]

SUSPICION CAN CREATE AN OVERWHELMING NEED TO be in control of every aspect of life. We become reluctant to turn over the reins, even for a minute. We question whether someone, or something, can do as well as we're doing on our own.

But asking for help is *not* a sign of weakness. It merely means that you're a realistic person. You see that you've exhausted your own resources and yet still haven't reached your goal. So you make the only reasonable choice: you look for assistance.

Complacency

"Why should I endeavor to ameliorate my writing skill? It appears to be satisfactory and/or copacetic."[4]

ANOTHER FORM OF SUSPICION IS THE TENDENCY TO be satisfied with the status quo, even when it leaves much to be desired. We doubt the importance of changing our habits and convince ourselves that our situation isn't so bad after all. Instead of being concerned or angry about our circumstance, we become unemotional and detached. We develop a kind of "tunnel vision" that enables us to focus only on the current project. We convince ourselves that it's just *one* letter, *one* memo, or *one* newsletter. We fail to see the cumulative effect of bad writing.

Only the power of Standard English can break the dependence on bad writing habits and enable us to see the quality of our prose objectively.

Embracing Step 3

THE THIRD STEP TOWARD RECOVERY WILL FREE YOU from the need to use suspicion as an excuse for not seeking help.

Step 3: Believe that Standard English can heal you.

Working through this step means acknowledging that your addiction to bad writing has become unmanageable by your own efforts. It means that, despite still having some questions and concerns, you're willing to give Standard English a chance. It means you're ready to begin relearning good grammar, effective syntax, and proper punctuation.

Others Have Changed

CHANGE IS POSSIBLE. OVER THE YEARS, I'VE MET many people who initially felt inadequate to the task, but who eventually overcame malescribism:

- Tom G., an architect who finally realized that he didn't need to manhandle English to feel strong and in control. Today his style is crisp and clean, and he's never felt more in command of his life and his ideas.
- Martha D., an attractive thirty-five year old who sensed that men didn't respect her. After working through the twelve steps and overcoming her sloppy grammar, she noticed a difference in the way she was treated. Now, she's happily married to a great guy (who is a recovered malescribe himself).
- Cathy W., who allowed her repressed memories of her parents' indifference to the language to affect her writing. Now she's moving ahead, making Standard English her own, and breaking the vicious cycle.

If positive change can happen to others, it can happen to you.

What's Ahead

YOU'RE NOW READY TO CONFRONT THE UNDERLYING causes of malescribism and learn how to *change* your bad writing habits. As you work through the remaining steps,

---

your commitment must be flexible enough to accommodate the inevitable mood swings, disappointments, and frustrations you will experience. After all, you're trying to overcome unresolved writing issues, social learning, and well-practiced psychological defenses. So pace yourself. Before long you'll be writing more clearly, confidently, and persuasively. And as your skills develop, you'll open doors to new personal and professional opportunities that depend on effective written communication skills.

Because of the difficulty of the process, you might want to keep these comforting items handy: a teddy bear; several pounds of chocolate; a favorite old sweater; vodka or scotch (not both); a box of tissues. Let's proceed.

Endnotes

1. "Who's" should be "whose."
2. Italics should be used instead of underlining. Never use more than one question mark.
3. The apostrophe is missing in "don't." The first sentence should be written as two sentences.
4. The "fancy" words—"ameliorate" and "copacetic"—should be replaced with simpler words.

STOP WRITING WEAK SENTENCES

(by Overcoming Insecurity)

NOW THAT YOU'VE WORKED THROUGH THE FIRST three steps of this program, you've created a solid foundation upon which to build your new writing life. You've admitted that bad writing exists. You've overcome your pride and learned that you are responsible for your recovery. And you've put your trust in Standard English. Now you're ready to begin actually changing your bad writing habits and overcoming malescribism. But first, let's look at just how deeply rooted these bad habits are.

The Origins of Bad Writing Habits

MALESCRIBISM IS A COMPLEX AFFLICTION THAT MAN-ifests itself in many ways. But the questionable techniques that malescribes use all have their roots in painful early childhood events.

As children, we all experienced writing traumas: humiliation after turning in a book report late; shame from getting a low grade on an essay assignment; feeling insignificant when parents dismissed our poetry with the comment, "That's nice, dear." Being defenseless and having no strategies for dealing with these traumas, we repressed them.

The person you were at the time of these early traumas is often referred to as your "inner child-writer." However, that part of your personality is not really "in the past." It is within you *now*. And it is still young, vulnerable, and needy. But because of the effectiveness of ego defense mechanisms, your inner child-writer was long ago silenced. So its needs have to be expressed in some other way.

We now know that malescribism represents an attempt to nurture that neglected inner child-writer. As Sigmund Freud should have said, writing "mistakes" are the means by which an adult's subconscious mind tries to meet long forgotten emotional needs.

When we were children, the primary givers/withholders of approval were our parents and other authority figures. But adult malescribes rationalize that their parents (dead or alive) can't possibly still be playing that role. So malescribes subconsciously assign the role to others—

their readers (or to use the technical term, "reader-parents"). And in trying to please them, malescribes display a fundamental sense of *insecurity*.

How Insecurity Works

INSECURITY IS ESSENTIALLY A FEAR OF THE UNFA-miliar. It is an overwhelming urge to avoid risk, stay with what's known, and find solace in comfortable habits.

Your inner child-writer still feels the need to seek safety. The way adult malescribes subconsciously express that need is to use familiar words and phrases. And they prefer indirect, self-effacing expressions that they hope won't seem discourteous. In other words, they write **weak sentences.**

Let's take a look at some specific techniques that malescribes use to avoid risk and decrease the possibility of offending their readers.

Stretching the Meanings of Words

"I know that my writing is somewhat uncreative, but it's very typical and fairly functional."[1]

MALESCRIBES WANT TO CONVEY SHADES OF MEAN-ing, just like everyone else. But instead of confidently selecting appropriate words, they often choose familiar words and try to make them do more than they realistically can. Consider the following sentence:

- After Biff fumbled the ball, his coach was _____ .

Healthy writers might use *livid* or *furious* to complete the sentence. But malescribes, seeing the writing process through their "insecurity filter," typically use *very angry,* even if they are aware of other options. To their minds, it is the safe, comfortable choice. The intensifiers *very, so,* and *extremely* work adequately to convey nuance, so they are used automatically. But they are an unhealthy crutch.

Malescribes also rely heavily on the qualifiers *rather, fairly,* and *somewhat.* Consider these examples:

- I called an ambulance because the injury seemed to be rather serious.
- Learning to play the sonata was a fairly challenging task.
- Smedley wasted no time in hiring a somewhat attractive secretary.

Notice how the qualifying words weaken the impact of the sentences by creating some uncertainty. How is *rather serious* different from *serious?* How does *fairly chal-*

lenging compare to *challenging?* And what, exactly, does *somewhat attractive* imply?

Excessive use of qualifiers also illustrates that malescribes like to show that they are in control of their affliction. So instead of trusting well-chosen words to do their jobs, they try to "help" less effective words by tacking on qualifiers.

HEALING TIP:

Choose suitably vivid words instead of stretching less appropriate words with qualifiers.

Downplaying Action

"When my words are being written, my concern is with the reaction that will be given by my readers."[2]

MALESCRIBES FEEL A STRONG NEED TO SHOW THAT they "know their place," so they try not to seem too independent or assertive. In an attempt to appear unassuming and respectful, and thereby win approval from their readers, they begin to rely on indirect expression. They prefer to use the *passive voice,* where the subject of the sentence is acted upon (as opposed to the *active voice,* where the subject performs an action). Here's an illustration of the technique:

- Tragically, hundreds of lives were lost when the iceberg was rammed by the ship.

Healthy writers see that the passive voice is inappropriate for describing such a dramatic, action-filled event. It shifts the emphasis away from the performer of the action. Therefore, *active-voice sentences* are usually preferable because they are more direct, energetic, and succinct. The previous example can be better written like this:

- Tragically, hundreds of people died when the ship rammed the iceberg.

Passive-voice construction can also create some confusion about responsibility. Take, for example, this instruction:

- At this point, the spreadsheet file should be saved.

Does this sentence mean that the file should already be saved (because of previous actions)? Or does it mean that the reader should (now) save the file? An active-voice sentence would eliminate the confusion:

- At this point, save the spreadsheet file.

Now the meaning of the instruction is clear.

THE **PASSIVE VOICE** IS APPROPRIATE IN CERTAIN cases. Here's an example where it works well:

- Following the concert, wine and cheese will be served in the lobby.

In this sentence it doesn't matter who will be serving the refreshments. The performer of the action isn't important, so the active voice isn't required. Now take a look at one more example:

- The wrecked cab had to be towed to a body shop.

Disclosing the identity of the actor (the tow truck driver) would add nothing to this sentence, so the passive voice is acceptable.

> **HEALING TIP:**
>
> Reserve the passive voice for sentences in which the actor is either unknown or unimportant.

Overusing Euphemisms

"I admit to being a grammatically challenged student, but I don't think my writing is, shall we say, self-conscious."[3]

IN AN EFFORT TO APPEAR POLITE AND DEFERENTIAL, malescribes typically will state ideas in a roundabout way. They worry that their readers might be displeased with direct prose that could be interpreted as crude, clumsy, tactless, or offensive. So malescribes often use euphemisms.

In the magical world of euphemisms, beggars become panhandlers, lies become categorical inaccuracies, and prisons become correctional facilities. In general, such polite rewording isn't a problem. It softens some of life's harsh realities but still conveys the intended meaning.

But malescribes, overly worried about offending people, often will carry euphemistic expression to extremes. For example, they might use euphemisms that are overly poetic *(green-eyed monster* for *envy)* or pretentious *(au na-turel* for *naked)*. Or they might use expressions that are self-consciously modest *(private parts* for *genitals)* or grandiose *(sanitation engineer* for *trash collector)*.

Malescribes also carry on the questionable tradition of "political correctness," an obsession with mollifying overly sensitive readers. So they readily use creations such as *weight enhanced, ethically impaired,* and *musically chal-lenged* when direct, less self-conscious words and phrases would be fine.

HEALING TIP:

Use euphemisms when they seem appropriate; but in general, try to express your thoughts di-rectly.

Running Sentences Together

"I'm trying to overcome my bad writing habits, there are so many of them that I'm not sure how to proceed."[4]

AFTER YEARS OF BLAND, UNORIGINAL WRITING, malescribes can begin to doubt their ability to keep their

·readers' attention. This fear of abandonment often motivates malescribes to run one sentence into the next. It's just another way of playing it safe.

Here's an example of the run-on technique:

• I offered her my jacket, she declined.

This sentence contains two independent clauses (grammatically complete clauses that could stand alone as sentences). Healthy writers know that two independent clauses can't be joined by a comma. The clauses need to be treated in one of three ways:

1. Rewrite them as two sentences:

• I offered her my jacket. She declined.

2. Separate them with a semicolon:

• I offered her my jacket; she declined.

3. Separate them with a comma and a conjunction *(or, and, but, for, nor, so,* or *yet):*

• I offered her my jacket, but she declined.

Sentence run-ons also can occur when connecting adverbs are used between independent clauses. Here's an example:

- We love our new house, however, it needs a lot of work.

Here, the run-on could be avoided by preceding the adverb *however* with a semicolon, as shown here:

- We love our new house; however, it needs a lot of work.

Other connecting adverbs to watch out for include *therefore, however, similarly, nevertheless, furthermore, then,* and *consequently.*

Certain transitional phrases can also create run-ons, as illustrated here:

- The fender was crushed, the frame was bent, and the windshield was broken, in other words, the car was heavily damaged.

Here, the phrase *in other words* creates the run-on. Other transitional phrases to be on the lookout for include *for example, as a result,* and *on the contrary.*

Failing to Be Original

"I'm working like a dog to improve my writing, but I always seem to end up back at square one. The crux of the matter is that I don't think I'm making much progress."[5]

AFTER YEARS OF LIVING IN THE FOG OF MALE-scribism, it's easy to rely on words and phrases that are familiar and safe. They won't offend or be misunderstood, so they become the addict's best friends.

Malescribes try to avoid risk by using clichés, unimaginative comparisons, and stale expressions. Below is a list of fifty of these widely used phrases. Do you see any of *your* favorites in the list?

after all is said and done
ahead of the game

at square one
at the end of my rope
beyond the call of duty
bottom line
burning the candle at both ends
carved in stone
clear as a bell
crux of the matter
cute as a button
dyed in the wool
easy as 1-2-3
equal to the task
every cloud has a silver lining
far and away the best
first and foremost
flat as a pancake
free as a bird
generous to a fault
happy as a clam
horns of a dilemma
in the final analysis
laundry list
like taking candy from a baby
living legend
once and for all
on the edge of my seat

on the same page
outside the box
over the hill
preaching to the choir
pretty as a picture
quick as a wink
quiet as a mouse
real-life superheroes
sang like an angel
selling like hotcakes
skeletons in the closet
slept like a baby
smart as a whip
smooth as silk
snowballed
solid as a rock
take a dim view of
through thick and thin
tough as nails
under the gun
worked like a dog
worst-case scenario

The ease with which malescribes use these hackneyed phrases is astounding. Therefore, an essential part of the recovery process is to condition the mind to sound an alarm whenever they emerge from your pen or keyboard. So you should read this list three times per week during the early stages of recovery. Purging these phrases from your repertoire will create the opportunity once again to engage your mind in *creating* prose, not merely copying or repeating it.

Some malescribes will even try to justify a timeworn phrase by indicating their awareness of it, as in this example:

- Excuse the cliché, but it was like taking candy from a baby.

This technique doesn't make the phrase any more effective. It simply indicates that the writer wasn't willing to recast the sentence in a fresh way.

HEALING TIP:

Avoid worn-out words and phrases, using instead fresh, creative expressions.

Avoiding the Issue

"I really don't think that my writing is weak. On the other hand, I guess it could use some improvement."[6]

UNDER THE INFLUENCE OF MALESCRIBISM, WRITERS often become uncertain of their own positions on issues because they are trying to meet the imagined expectations of every possible reader. As a result, their sentences can reflect a lack of confidence and purpose. Here's an illustration:

> • I feel strongly that the time has come for us to adopt the resolution. But many others feel strongly that the committee should consider alternatives, and I can certainly understand their point.

Malescribes fear criticism from others who *might* be more informed, confident, or assertive. They don't want to take the chance of offending anyone by appearing disrespectful or overconfident. So they meekly walk the fine line between expressing their own views and accommodating opposing views. The result is prose that lacks force and persuasiveness.

State your opinions clearly, confidently, and without equivocation.

Embracing Step 4

THE FOURTH STEP TOWARD RECOVERY WILL FREE you from the need to write cautiously, indirectly, and uncreatively.

Step 4: Stop writing weak sentences.

In working through this step, you're declaring your independence from writing techniques that are motivated by the need for safety. You're giving yourself permission to take a little risk. You're saying that you no longer will waste your present writing moments trying to find ways to stay in your comfort zone.

To eliminate weak sentences, just follow this chapter's healing tips:

- Choose suitably vivid words instead of stretching less appropriate words with qualifiers.

- Reserve the passive voice for sentences in which the actor is either unknown or unimportant.
- Use euphemisms when they seem appropriate; but in general, try to express your thoughts directly.
- Avoid running sentences together by using appropriate punctuation or by writing two separate sentences.
- Avoid worn-out words and phrases, using instead fresh, creative expressions.
- State your opinions clearly, confidently, and without equivocation.

What's Ahead

AS YOU WORK THROUGH THE REMAINING EIGHT steps, you'll learn about other repressed emotional needs that are responsible for bad writing decisions. You'll have opportunities to reconnect with your neglected inner child-writer and move forward toward recovery. It's the only way to reintegrate your fragmented psyche and overcome malescribism for good. It really is.

Endnotes

1. "Somewhat," "very," and "fairly" should be replaced with stronger words.

2. "Are being written" and "will be given" should be replaced with active-voice phrases.

3. "Grammatically-challenged" and "shall we say" make the writer seem self-conscious.

4. This sentence should be written as two sentences.

5. Three clichés in two consecutive sentences are too many!

6. The second sentence weakens the first.

STOP WRITING FORMAL SENTENCES

(by Overcoming Worry)

"WHAT WILL OTHERS THINK ABOUT MY WRITING style? Am I using the right words? Will people take me seriously?" While healthy writers are busy putting their well-organized thoughts on paper, malescribes question their own judgment and wonder what others will think. They imagine reactions from their readers ranging from indifference to disapproval to rejection. The underlying problem is *worry*, one of the most immobilizing emotions. Worry inhibits spontaneous, engaging writing and can lead to questionable decisions about grammar and style.

Everybody in recovery once was consumed with worry about making good writing choices. Ted M. is no exception.

Ted's Bout with Worry

AFTER MANY YEARS IN THE GRIP OF MALESCRIBISM, Ted M. finally admitted his addiction to bad writing and was on his way to verbal enlightenment. But worry stood in the way of his progress. Here's the way Ted described his problem:

In my work at an architectural firm, I occasionally have to write memos, reports, and proposals. Until recently, those tasks caused me a great deal of anxiety. Although I knew what I needed to say, I usually had lots of trouble getting it down on paper.

I worried about what my coworkers would think about me. If I used a vivid word, would I seem pretentious? If I tried to be creative, would they think I was showing off? If I tried to make a point, would it come across as too pushy? The list of concerns went on and on. I became so tentative that I would spend hours on the simplest writing project. I started having frequent headaches, and I began losing weight.

After embracing Standard English and talking with other recovering malescribes, I began to understand what I had been doing. I know now that I was equating worrying with caring. *I thought that by checking my own decisions against what I guessed my readers expected, I was showing them how much I valued their opinions. Of course, in doing so, I devalued my own ideas, weakening my prose and further contributing to my indecisiveness and feelings of inferiority. I just wanted to measure up. I just wanted to be accepted.*

The Nature of Worry

TED'S DISCLOSURE SUGGESTS THAT WORRY IS AN ATtempt to avert disapproval by *someone* that *might* be given at *some* time in the future. This type of thinking prevents malescribes from living in the present writing-moment and attending to the task at hand. Most of their energy is spent speculating about how their readers will judge their competency, instead of honing a clear and persuasive message.

Your inner child-writer feels the need to impress others. It wants desperately to be patted on the back for being "all grown up." So the way adult malescribes subconsciously express this compulsion is by adopting an affected, stilted writing style. They try to measure up to a high but vague standard. In other words, they write **formal sentences.**

Let's take a look at some specific techniques that malescribes use to appear mature and polished, and thereby win favor from their readers.

Using Pretentious Language

"I always endeavor to utilize multisyllabic words. It is the manner in which sophisticated people write."[1]

ONE TECHNIQUE FAVORED BY MALESCRIBES IS TO USE fancy words where simpler words would be appropriate. It is an attempt to show how hard they are trying and how competent they have become.

Here's a short list of fancy words that malescribes love to use, along with their simpler alternatives:

Fancy word	*Alternative*
altercation	fight
ameliorate	improve
appellation	name
capacious	roomy
cogitate	think
confabulate	chat
diminution	decrease
domicile	home
edifice	building
egress	exit

Fancy word	*Alternative*
facilitate	aid
impecunious	poor
intermix	mix
jocular	witty
masticate	chew
modification	change
pedagogue	teacher
perambulate	stroll
prevaricator	liar
procure	buy
prognosticate	predict
pulchritude	beauty
pusillanimous	timid
recapitulation	summary
remuneration	payment
salubrious	healthful
sobriquet	nickname
somnolent	sleepy
terminate	end
utilize	use
verisimilitude	authenticity
vicissitude	hardship
vociferate	shout

High-sounding words like these suggest that one's ideas aren't interesting on their own and therefore need to be "enhanced." But malescribes, seeing the writing process through their "worry filter," don't recognize this faulty reasoning. They are focused on drawing attention and trying to impress their readers with their verbal skills.

HEALING TIP:

Avoid using large and pretentious words when simple ones will do.

Detaching Yourself from Your Writing

"This observer feels that formal style is more likely to be accepted by educated and influential people."[2]

HEALTHY WRITERS KNOW THAT IT'S FINE TO REFER to oneself as *I*. But malescribes feel more comfortable referring to themselves in the third person. They prefer *this observer, the author,* or *the present writer* because they see such expressions as being more dignified and serious than a personal pronoun. This kind of formality represents an attempt to appear cultivated and elicit favorable reactions from readers.

Notice how easily one can run into difficulties when applying this misguided technique:

- When this writer began this piece, this writer felt that this writer's obligation was to present both sides of the issue.

This sentence is unnecessarily clumsy. By using personal pronouns, we can create a more natural-sounding sentence, as shown below:

- When I began this piece, I felt that my obligation was to present both sides of the issue.

By dissociating the "personal self" and the "writer self," you lose your authority and the power of your own voice. But by using the first person when appropriate, you can become whole again.

HEALING TIP:

Don't detach yourself from your writing by referring to yourself in the third person.

Avoiding Contractions

"I do not think my writing is too formal. I will wager that it is as clear as anyone's. Do you not agree?"[3]

TO APPEAR EDUCATED AND BE TAKEN SERIOUSLY, malescribes often shy away from using contractions. They fear a negative reaction by readers who might see an informal writing style as being unrefined or careless. So malescribes create sentences that are unnecessarily stiff.

Consider this sentence from an interoffice memo:

- Let us talk at 9:00 tomorrow in the boardroom. If you will not be able to make it, please let me know, and I will reschedule for Friday.

Now look at a less formal version:

- Let's talk at 9:00 tomorrow in the boardroom. If you won't be able to make it, please let me know, and I'll reschedule for Friday.

The second sentence is just as "serious" as the first— and more effective. Contractions make the sentences less choppy and more like conversational speech.

For most types of factual writing, contractions can be used effectively, as long as they aren't so numerous as to become distracting to readers.

Misusing Personal Pronouns

"This 12-step program has given myself hope!"[4]

IN THE MUDDLED MINDS OF MALESCRIBES, WRITING is a means of earning approval. As a result, they often will go to great lengths to appear modest and unassuming, hoping that their readers will look upon them favorably.

One tendency is to avoid using the pronoun *me* to refer to oneself, even when it is correct. Consider the following sentence, which uses a personal pronoun *(me)* to refer to the writer:

• The award was given to my partner and me.

Enlightened writers will recognize that the sentence is correct. But in the minds of malescribes, *me* doesn't appear "refined," so they incorrectly will use either *I* or *myself,* as in these sentences:

- The award was given to my partner and I.
- The award was given to my partner and me.

Healthy writing demands that you use appropriate pronouns. So how do you decide whether *I*, *me*, or *myself* is correct? You need to ask a simple question: Are you the *subject* or the *object*? In other words, are you acting, or are you being acted upon?

If you are the *subject*, use the pronoun I. (If someone else is the subject, use *he, she, we*, or *they*.)

But if you are the *object*, use *me*, as shown in these examples.

- The ball hit me in the head.
- Georgette drove Harold and me to the airport.
- My attorney agreed to meet with me tomorrow.
- The present was meant for you and me.

In the first two examples, the pronoun is the object of a verb, and in the last two, the pronoun is the object of a preposition.* (If someone else is the object, use *him, her, us*, or *them*.)

---

*Frequently used prepositions include *about, after, against, at, beside, by, except, for, from, in, of, on, over*, and *to*.

The exception occurs when you are both the subject and the object, as shown here:

- I cut myself while shaving.

Here, the person acting is also the person being acted upon. (When others are involved, use *he. . . himself, she . . . herself, they . . . themselves,* or *we . . . ourselves.*

HEALING TIP:

When you are the *subject,* use *I;* when you are the *object* only, use *me;* and when you are both the *subject and the object,* use *myself.*

Using the Subjunctive Mood Indiscriminately

"Since I've started this twelve-step program, I believe that my writing be better than ever."[5]

THE SUBJUNCTIVE MOOD IS USED TO EXPRESS *wishes* or *hypothetical situations.* And malescribes, even if they aren't sure of the rules, often can get it right. For example, they might realize the need for the present-tense subjunctive in this sentence:

• I wish I were a millionaire.

It's clear that to write "I wish I was a millionaire" would be wrong because it would refer to a wish about the *past*. So the present-tense subjunctive is the obvious choice.

Most malescribes probably have encountered many examples of the subjunctive mood in print. For example, they might be familiar with this statement by Patrick Henry:

• "If this be treason, make the most of it."

But in an effort to appear in command of the technique, they might begin applying it haphazardly, as in this example:

• If this be meatloaf, then I question its preparation.

Although this sentence is grammatically correct, it will look odd to most people. When using the subjunctive, you should be guided by meaning and popular usage. If the sentence looks unusual and isn't what most people would say, you should rewrite it.

Common usage indicates where the subjunctive seems natural and not affected. Here are two phrases that are used frequently:

- I wouldn't do that if I were you.
- I move that the meeting be adjourned.

These expressions have become idiomatic and don't come across as being pretentious or self-consciously erudite.

Keep in mind that not all "if" statements are hypothetical. Take this sentence, for example:

- If Joan is late, she will miss the bus.

Here the statement is about something that may occur (in the future), so the subjunctive mood is not appropriate.

> **HEALING TIP:**
>
> Use the subjunctive mood when expressing wishes or hypothetical situations—unless it causes a sentence to seem unusual or affected.

Using Foreign Phrases

"It's de rigueur *to include a few foreign phrases in one's writing,* n'est-ce pas?*"*[6]

SUBCONSCIOUSLY, MALESCRIBES WRITE TO MEET repressed emotional needs. To appear sophisticated and worldly, they often drop foreign words and phrases into sentences for no apparent reason.

What language do malescribes prefer? Portuguese? Hungarian? No, they insist on French. To their minds, "casual" use of French suggests a sophistication that, for some reason, English cannot achieve.

Here are a few of the most commonly used phrases, along with their English equivalents:

French phrase	English equivalent
au naturel	naked
bon mot	witticism
de rigueur	customary
c'est la vie	that's life
coup de grâce	finishing blow
crème de la crème	the best
en masse	as a group
en plein air	outdoors
fait accompli	accomplished task

French phrase	*English equivalent*
je ne sais quoi	special something
mon ami	my friend
n'est-ce pas?	isn't it so?
objet d'art	work of art
sangfroid	composure
savoir faire	sophistication
vis-à-vis	in relation to

Enlightened writers will use French only if it conveys a meaning that isn't better expressed in English. So they have no qualms about using phrases such as *avant-garde, bon voyage, cul de sac,* and *hors d'oeuvre.* These phrases are not used to impress; rather, they are legitimate, useful terms unto themselves.

HEALING TIP:

Before using a foreign phrase, make sure your thought couldn't be expressed better in English.

Embracing Step 5

THE FIFTH STEP TOWARD RECOVERY WILL FREE YOU from the need to prove your sophistication with pretentious and stuffy language.

Step 5: Stop writing formal sentences.

In working through this step, you're deciding that your writing no longer will be about appearances. You're saying that you no longer will devote yourself to impressing your readers and getting their approval for your sophistication. From this day forward, your writing will be about communicating ideas clearly and confidently.

To eliminate formal sentences, follow this chapter's healing tips:

- Avoid using large and pretentious words when simple ones will do.
- Don't detach yourself from your writing by referring to yourself in the third person.
- Don't be afraid of using contractions judiciously in your writing.
- When you, the writer, are the *subject* of a sentence, use the pronoun *I;* when you are the *object,* use the pronoun *me.*

- Use the subjunctive mood when expressing wishes or hypothetical situations—unless it causes a sentence to seem unusual or affected.
- Before using a foreign phrase, make sure your thought couldn't be expressed better in English.

By the way, if you now feel the need to apologize to those people you've hurt with your writing over the years, go right ahead.

Endnotes

1. The pretentious words—"endeavor" and "utilize"—could be replaced with "try" and "use."
2. Referring to yourself as "this observer" is overly formal and dated.
3. The absence of contractions makes this sentence seem formal.
4. "Myself" should be "me."
5. The subjunctive isn't appropriate here because the situation described isn't hypothetical ("be" should be "is").
6. The two French phrases come across as unnecessary and pretentious.

STEP 6

STOP WRITING
OVERWEIGHT SENTENCES

(by Overcoming Shame)

IN THE PREVIOUS TWO CHAPTERS, WE LOOKED AT *IN-security,* which is the basis for safe, tentative sentences, and *worry,* which can lead to weak sentences. Now let's examine *shame,* another emotion that leads malescribes to use approval-seeking techniques in their writing.

Shame is a painful psychological state brought about by awareness of some real or imagined guilt, shortcoming, or impropriety. Subconsciously, it motivates us to build psychic walls that can protect our egos from further insults. Shame can affect all aspects of life, including writing. Let's learn more about it.

How Shame Develops

AS CHILDREN, WE WERE JUDGED BY PARENTS, teachers, and other writing critics. And those judgments are still with us, existing in a repressed state and outside conscious thinking. But in supportive therapy groups, subconscious memories can often "bubble to the surface" and be examined.

In one such group participants were asked to recall a particularly shaming statement that wounded them during their early years. After many tearful moments, here's what they had to say:

- Aaron: "Why can't you write more like your sister?"
- Barb: "Perhaps you'd like to share your little joke about colons with the whole class."
- Chadsworth: "And just where did you learn that word, young man?"
- Lorenzo: "A 'C' in Composition? Well, I hope you're happy."
- Martha: "Okay, punctuate it your way. I'm just your mother."

What these people wanted as children—what we all wanted—were words of encouragement and acceptance.

We wanted our efforts at writing to be acknowledged by significant adults. But what we got too often were implicit messages of disapproval and dissatisfaction: "You're not doing it correctly," "You're not good enough," or, "You're embarrassing us."

Because we didn't know how to fend off such messages, we internalized them. We came to believe that *we* were responsible for causing others to be disappointed. We felt as if we had let down the adults by not meeting their expectations. So we experienced feelings of worthlessness and shame.

Your inner child-writer is still feeling the shame. It just wants to be protected and be accepted. And the way adult malescribes subconsciously seek this protection is with wordiness that serves as a kind of psychic buffer against potentially stinging remarks by their readers. In other words, they write **overweight sentences.**

Let's look at some techniques that malescribes use to protect themselves from further disapproval and criticism.

Using Wordy Phrases

"In spite of the fact that I'm very liberal in my use of words, I believe that I write in an effective manner."[1]

OVER TIME, MALESCRIBES OFTEN BEGIN TO EQUATE quantity with quality, and they come to fear that concise sentences might not satisfy their readers. As a result, they often rely on wordy phrases to give their sentences an "adequate" length.

Here is a short list of wordy phrases that malescribes typically use.

Wordy phrase	*Concise equivalent*
after the conclusion of	after
at this point in time	at this time; now
be in possession of	possess; have
by means of	by
despite the fact that	despite
during the course of	during
filled with anger	angry
for the simple reason that	because
in an effective manner	effectively
in a state of confusion	confused
in a timely manner	promptly
in order to	to
in spite of the fact that	although
in the event that	if
is indicative of	indicates
it is often the case that	frequently
on a weekly basis	weekly
on the order of	about

Wordy phrase	*Concise equivalent*
owing to the fact that	because
take into consideration	consider
until such time	until
with the exception of	except for

Notice that the extra words don't add anything of significance. The wordy phrases are no more serious, compelling, or informative than their concise alternatives.

But malescribes, looking through their "shame filter," believe that using extra words makes their sentences seem more substantial. As with most unhealthy writing techniques, this one backfires. Wordy phrases actually suggest that the sentences are "thin" in meaning. They suggest that the writer is padding the prose—compensating for some deficiency.

HEALING TIP:

When tempted to use a wordy phrase, choose a concise alternative instead.

Writing Long Sentences

"The fact of the matter is that my writing is improving slowly for the simple reason that old habits are hard to break."[2]

ANOTHER WAY TO ADD BULK TO WRITING IS TO CRE-ate unnecessarily long sentences. This technique is particularly popular with malescribes who work in law, government, insurance, and the social sciences.

Using a lot of words provides a safety margin. In the minds of malescribes, more words create more protection from error or judgment. If some words don't work, maybe the others will.

Here's an example of this misguided technique:

- The hospital received the needed money from two people who decided not to disclose their identities.

An enlightened writer would be more likely to write the sentence this way:

- The hospital received the needed money from two anonymous donors.

Concise sentences have a force that wordy sentences don't have. Extraneous words merely take up space and dilute the impact of the idea being expressed.

Now take a look at two more wordy examples:

- Consuming excessive calories at breakfast, lunch, and dinner can lead to an increase in blood pressure.
- Owing to the fact that my car is not the most reliable of machines, I often show up for appointments after their scheduled commencement times.

Now notice how the same ideas can be expressed in more direct sentences with fewer words:

- Overeating at meals can increase blood pressure.
- Because my car is unreliable, I am often late for appointments.

For malescribes, each extraneous word fortifies the sentence and strengthens the barrier between their egos and potential criticism. But healthy writing demands a cleaner, more concise approach.

Relying on "Fine" Writing

"Each time I apply pen to paper, I try to be creative in my use of the King's English."[3]

FINE WRITING IS A FACETIOUS TERM THAT DEscribes ornate and inexplicably poetic writing. Although it appears pompous and artificial, malescribes love it. It's another way of creating overweight sentences that provide the emotional protection they crave. It's also the malescribe's way of saying to readers, "Notice how clever I am!"

Here are some examples of the technique, along with their more direct alternatives:

"Fine" phrase	*Unpretentious alternative*
amorous tête-à-tête	affair
as Old Sol began to ascend	at sunrise

"Fine" phrase	*Unpretentious alternative*
at the stroke of midnight	at midnight
consumed the evening repast	ate dinner
digging implement	shovel
engaged the services of	hired
entered this veil of tears	was born
in the year of our Lord	in
it is the opinion of the author	I believe
oceangoing leviathan	ship
penned the scholarly tome	wrote the textbook
pugilistic spectacle	boxing match
the pigskin sport	football
these United States	the United States
wandering celestial orbs	planets
white flaky precipitation	snow

There's no doubt that this kind of phrasing *is* creative. There's also no doubt that it's out of place in most types of writing. It suggests a world too unlike the everyday world that most of us inhabit. So recovering malescribes should strive to overcome the need to use flowery, poetic phrases.

Creating Unwieldy Noun Strings

"Sentence punctuation utilization is probably my biggest problem." [4]

WE ALL KNOW THAT NOUNS CAN BE USED AS ADJECtives, as in this example:

- Roger's car radio was always set on Oldies 105.

Here, the noun *car* functions as an adjective and modifies *radio*. This technique can be extended by stringing nouns together, as illustrated here:

- The sofa cushion springs were beginning to show signs of wear.

Here, *springs* is modified by two nouns: *sofa* and *cushion*. This technique generally makes a sentence more

---

concise. Without the noun string, one would need to write the sentence as follows:

- The springs contained in the sofa cushions were beginning to show signs of wear.

Noun strings generally are not a problem unless they get out of control—which they often do in the hands of male-scribes. Take a look at an example of noun string abuse:

- You will be visited each Friday by a patient treatment outcome evaluation team.

Here, *team* is modified by *patient treatment outcome evaluation*—four nouns in succession! Long noun strings can create confusion and cause readers to backtrack. So it's usually a good idea to reword such sentences to make them easier to understand. Here's an effective revision of the previous example:

- Each Friday a team will visit you to evaluate the outcome of your treatment.

Not only is this version easier to understand, it's also in the active voice.

Before leaving the topic, let's look at a few more examples of hideous too long noun strings:

- Next, locate the computer peripheral interface cable connector.
- The hog farm equipment leasing industry is rebounding after three slow quarters.
- Drum unit corona wire cleaning is required when you replace the toner cartridge in your printer.
- The director will oversee the Deployable Communications Systems Integration Support program.

Stringing nouns together can give malescribes a "high" that makes them feel powerful and in control. But it's all an illusion. True verbal power is conveyed only by clear, concise, direct sentences. So long nouns strings have to be eliminated.

HEALING TIP:

Don't create unwieldy noun strings.

Being Pointlessly Redundant

"I think that a certain amount of repetitive redundancy helps to get my point across."[5]

HEALTHY WRITERS KNOW THAT REDUNDANCY CAN BE an effective and emphatic tool when used judiciously. But malescribes often use it indiscriminately as yet another emotional crutch.

Take a look at a short list of redundant phrases that malescribes find appealing:

Redundant phrase	*Concise equivalent*
absolutely necessary	necessary
advance warning	warning
basic fundamentals	fundamentals
close scrutiny	scrutiny
extremely unique	unique
final outcome	outcome
future plans	plans
honest truth	truth
joint collaboration	collaboration
join together	join
overused cliché	cliché
past history	history
regular routine	routine

Redundant phrase	Concise equivalent
repeat again	repeat
safe haven	haven
share in common	share
sudden impulse	impulse
totally unanimous	unanimous
ultimate outcome	outcome
unexpected surprise	surprise
whether or not	whether

You can see in this list that nothing is contributed by the redundant word or words. For example, the only kind of *truth* is *honest truth,* and everyone knows it. With this technique, malescribes are qualifying words that don't need qualifying. They are trying to exert control over the words because they don't trust the words to do their jobs.

HEALING TIP:

Don't use pointlessly redundant phrases.

Including Deadwood

"At this point in time, the words I use might be large in number, but I don't see that as a problem to be solved."[6]

ANOTHER WAY MALESCRIBES CREATE OVERWEIGHT sentences is to include *deadwood*—words and phrases that seem to add clarification but really don't. Here are some examples of sentences containing deadwood (indicated by brackets):

- [To get right to the point,] I'd like to announce my opposition to the plan.
- Where is the manuscript [at]?
- At this [point in] time, we need to proceed cautiously.
- At the end of the street was an abandoned house [that nobody lived in].
- We gazed at the silver moon [up in the sky].
- I can't believe the way [in which] Jill writes.
- [The truth is that] Jack likes to bet on basketball games.
- Susan wore an attractive suit that was navy blue [in color].
- Their weekend cabin was comfortable despite being small [in size].

- Corrine won the competition because her solo was the best [of all].
- Peter's agent always took 10 percent [of the total].
- Dr. Greene's biography [about the life] of Albert Schweitzer has become a bestseller.
- One of Johnny's chores was to empty [out] the trash.

As you can see, the deadwood states what is obvious and undeniable. It merely adds clutter to sentences. So why do malescribes love to include it? It's a relatively easy way to add an extra layer of protection from possible shaming remarks by their readers. And it gives malescribes some satisfaction in knowing that they can't be criticized for being lazy or incomplete.

HEALING TIP:

Eliminate the deadwood from your sentences.

Embracing Step 6

THE SIXTH STEP TOWARD RECOVERY WILL FREE YOU from the need to avoid direct, concise expression of your ideas.

Step 6: Stop writing overweight sentences.

In working through this step, you're making a decision to use your writing to communicate, not to shield yourself from imagined criticism. You're deciding that your writing doesn't have to be about showing those early childhood critics how far you've come. It doesn't have to ask for approval.

To eliminate overweight sentences, follow the healing tips presented in this chapter:

- When tempted to use a wordy phrase, choose a concise alternative instead.
- Make sentences as concise as possible by eliminating unnecessary words and phrases.
- When confronted with the urge to use flowery phrases, instead choose simpler, less pretentious phrases.
- Don't create unwieldy noun strings.

- Don't use pointlessly redundant phrases.
- Eliminate the deadwood from your sentences.

Endnotes

1. "In spite of the fact" and "in an effective manner" are wordy phrases.
2. "Of the matter" could be deleted. "For the simple reason that" could be replaced with "because."
3. "Apply pen to paper" and "the King's English" should be replaced with less poetic words. Also, "the King's English" refers to British usage.
4. "Sentence punctuation utilization" is an awkward noun string.
5. "Repetitive redundancy" is unnecessarily redundant!
6. "In time," "in number," and "to be solved" add nothing and should be deleted.

STOP WRITING UNCLEAR SENTENCES

(by Overcoming Indifference)

HEALTHY WRITERS HAPPILY COOPERATE WITH READERS, providing everything necessary for comprehension. But malescribes often withhold the words and elaboration necessary for correct interpretation. It's as if they are saying, "*I* know what I mean, so you should, too—regardless of how I write my sentences." In other words, malescribes display *indifference* to the requirements of clear and complete writing. How does this lack of concern originate?

The Roots of Indifference

DURING THE FIRST FEW YEARS OF LIFE, WE COMmunicated with cries, gurgles, and one- and two-word sentences. The remarkable thing was that our parents seemed to understand our intentions. They knew exactly what we meant and patiently supplied our needs. The world revolved around us: we wanted what we wanted, and that's all that mattered to us. We were self-absorbed and carefree, and our parents patiently tolerated our ego-centrism. They were compelled to take responsibility in every situation.

But all too soon our parents began making it known that our conception of the world was inadequate. They expected us to learn to be more responsible and to take other people's feelings and needs into account. And our initial response was, in effect, "Where's the payoff?" We had never cared much about others, so why should we change? We were indifferent to the pressure from our parents and tried to remain carefree as long as possible.

Your neglected inner child-writer still wants a life without accountability. It wants to satisfy its own needs while others gladly take responsibility. So adult male-scribes subconsciously express this desire by creating sentences that *they* understand but that lack adequate cues that would help other people understand. They create confusion and force their readers to guess at what was intended. In other words, they write **unclear sentences.**

The Effects of Indifference

THE CONNECTION BETWEEN EARLY LIFE EVENTS AND the emotions that underlie bad writing comes as a surprise to most recovering malescribes. Mindy L. was no exception.

Mindy L. is a high-school art teacher in a large midwestern city. For years she had struggled to overcome her questionable writing habits. But it was only when she decided to follow the twelve-step program that she was able to make progress. Here's what she had to say:

> *I was always tense when I wrote, and I couldn't figure out why. But after working through the initial steps of the recovery program, I gained some insight. I found out that my writing wasn't about communicating—it was about disregarding my readers' wishes. They merely wanted me to be mature and follow a few commonsense guidelines; but I was refusing, and my resistance was affecting my entire body. Once I became aware of the inner turmoil, I was able to start the healing and begin assuming responsibility for my sentences. As I gave up my need to control my readers, my whole body felt lighter and more flexible.*

Mindy overcame her need to let indifference guide her writing decisions—and so can you.

Let's examine some of the techniques that malescribes rely on to compel their readers to assume responsibility for the clarity of what they read.

Making Vague References

"My husband mentioned my grammar problems to my brother-in-law, and he was upset."[1]

HEALTHY WRITERS KNOW THAT A PRONOUN MUST refer clearly to some previous sentence element—the *antecedent*—to be understood. Here's an example of a correctly written sentence:

- Walter had worked hard all year, so he was looking forward to a vacation at the beach.

Here, the pronoun *he* clearly refers to *Walter*. Readers have been given all of the information they need to understand the sentence.

But malescribes, seeing the writing process through their "indifference filter," often use pronouns that aren't unambiguously linked to their antecedents. They simply don't care that their sentences will most likely be misinterpreted.

Three kinds of pronouns create the opportunity for error:

- Personal pronouns *(he, she, it, his, her, its)*
- Relative pronouns *(who, whom, which, that)*
- Demonstrative pronouns *(this, that, these, those)*

First, let's look at an example of the ambiguous reference technique involving a *personal* pronoun:

- Beth wanted to go shopping with Kathy, but she was too busy.

The question left in the reader's mind is: *who* was too busy? Was it Beth, or was it Kathy? There's no way to tell. Now let's examine a sentence whose problem lies in the careless use of a *relative* pronoun:

- Frank got married to Joyce in August, which was probably a mistake.

What was a mistake? Frank's getting married? Or his marrying Joyce? Or doing it in August? The antecedent of *which* isn't determinable in this sentence. We simply don't know what the writer had in mind.

And finally let's take a look at an example where a *demonstrative* pronoun has no clear antecedent:

- Greg's partner ordered a new computer and then took a two-hour lunch. This made Greg furious.

To what does *This* refer? Ordering the new computer? Taking a two-hour lunch? Or both? The meaning of the second sentence could be made clear by making a minor change, as shown here:

- Greg's partner ordered a new computer and then took a two-hour lunch. This long lunch break made Greg furious.

It's important to understand that people aren't mind readers. They can work only with the words they see on the page in front of them. So recovering malescribes have to become aware of the critical nature of the pronoun-antecedent relationship.

> **HEALING TIP:**
>
> When using a pronoun, make sure that its antecedent is obvious.

Substituting "Etc." for Explicit Phrases

"I'm pretty good at writing letters, e-mails, etc. So what more do I need to learn?"[2]

MALESCRIBES RELY ON BAD WRITING HABITS THAT leave questions in the minds of their readers. One such habit is the tendency to use the Latin phrase *et cetera,* abbreviated *etc.,* to mean *and others of the same kind.* Here is an illustration of the technique:

- Popular fonts are Times, Palatino, Bodoni, Schoolbook, etc.

What, exactly, does *etc.* represent here? What if the reader doesn't know any other fonts? The implicit message from the writer is: "I don't know, or don't care, what goes here. Maybe you have some ideas."

Notice how a simple change can eliminate the uncertainty:

- Popular fonts include Times, Palatino, Bodoni, and Schoolbook.

Now there's no obligation to refer to other (unnamed) examples of fonts. The uncertainty has been removed, and the sentence is clear.

Even more troubling is the use of more than one *etc.,* as illustrated here:

- In college, I took courses in psychology, sociology, philosophy, etc., etc.

Not only is *etc., etc.* uninformative, it's redundant as well. It also suggests that the writer is bored with the material being presented. Malescribes should strive to eliminate *etc.* from their sentences (as well as its equally vague English counterparts: the phrase *and so forth* and the phrase *and others*).

> **HEALING TIP:**
>
> Don't use *etc.* or any other uninformative word or phrase.

Using Lazy Words

"I feel fine about the progress I'm making in this nice twelve-step program."[3]

MALESCRIBES OFTEN INCLUDE VAPID WORDS THAT lack force and clarity, leaving readers with the responsibility of interpreting those words. Here's an example of this technique:

- The weather wasn't so good last week, so Jake and Veronica had to postpone their skiing trip.

What, exactly, is weather that's *not so good?* Is it too hot or too cold? Too rainy or or too dry? Too cloudy or too clear? When malescribes rely on lazy words, they subconsciously are trying to make their readers become editors.

Here's another example:

- James gave an awesome presentation at our weekly meeting.

Here, what are we to understand? Was the presentation James's best so far? Was it a crowd pleaser? Was it complete in every way? We can't be certain. We can conclude only that the writer is giving a positive assessment of the presentation.

Below is a list of words and phrases used frequently by malescribes, despite their uncertain implications. Do you see any of your favorites?

all right
awesome
awful
bogus
cute
fair
fine
good

great

gross

hot

lousy

neat

nice

nifty

not bad

okay

super

terrible

The problem with these words and phrases is that they don't convey an exact meaning. They are used merely to express the writer's general approval or disapproval.

A related technique that also creates uncertainty is the use of "not un——." Here's an example:

- Jack's contribution to the department during the past year was not unimpressive.

Here, *not unimpressive* doesn't really give a clear idea of the value of Jack's contribution. Was it only slightly better than nothing? Or was it a significant contribution? Or was its value somewhere between the two extremes? We're left to wonder.

Recovering malescribes should keep in mind that they need to choose words that convey a particular, understandable meaning.

HEALING TIP:

Avoid using lazy words that merely express your approval or disapproval.

Making Incomplete Comparisons

"These twelve steps are too difficult, and I'm too busy."[4]

MALESCRIBES, BELIEVING THAT THEIR READERS WILL tolerate sloppiness, often begin a thought without completing it. In other words, they shirk their responsibility as writers and compel their readers to guess at what is intended.

Here are some examples:

• Mortimer knew that he was too short.

Too short for what?

• More business people prefer our courier service.

More than what?

- Unfortunately, Kate's qualifications for the management position were less impressive.

Less impressive than what?

In each of these examples, the writer has provided no reference or baseline. No legitimate comparisons are being made, so the sentences can't be understood. Recovering malescribes must overcome the tendency to withhold the words that would make comparisons meaningful and clear.

HEALING TIP:

Whenever you make a comparison, be sure to include some kind of reference.

Using Unexplained Acronyms

"I don't know how much longer I can keep my malescribism a secret from the NCTE."[5]

IN AN *ACRONYM*, EACH LETTER REPRESENTS A WORD. For example, *HMO* stands for "Health Maintenance Organization." When healthy writers use an acronym, they automatically explain its meaning. But malescribes, subconsciously gripped by indifference, will often refuse to release that critical bit of information to their readers.

Here's an example:

- A representative of the ACLJ said that a formal statement would be given at the end of the week.

This sentence makes sense if readers know what *ACLJ* represents. But what if they don't?

The correct way to introduce an acronym is to show it in parentheses after the complete phrase, as shown here:

- A representative of the American Center for Law and Justice (ACLJ) said that a formal statement would be given at the end of the week.

Subsequently, the acronym can be presented alone. However, in a long work such as a book, it's a good idea to redefine acronyms occasionally (in case someone decides to read chapters out of sequence).

Some acronyms don't require such treatment. For example, it hardly matters what *NBC* represents because that network identifies itself as NBC (and rarely as the National Broadcasting Company). Other acronyms, such as *FBI* and *CIA,* are understood by most readers and therefore don't have to be explained.

Malescribes in recovery should keep in mind this simple guideline about acronyms: if there might be a doubt, write it out.

Using Jargon

"I'm not so sure I accept the psychogenic explanation of malescribism."[6]

PROFESSIONS AND ORGANIZATIONS FREQUENTLY make use of *jargon,* specialized words and phrases that simplify communication. When understood, it is an economical and clear means of exchanging ideas. But when used cavalierly in a nonspecialized context, jargon can create uncertainty in the minds of readers.

For example, *recession* has a specific definition and shouldn't be used to describe an apparent slowdown in the economy. Similarly, words from the social sciences, such as *schizophrenic, psychotic,* and *sociopathic,* have specialized meanings and aren't suitable for use in most writing.

Jargon can also find its way into sentences if it looks similar to an intended word. Here's an example:

- The criticality of the school's financial problems forced the administration to reduce faculty salaries.

The word *criticality* is jargon used exclusively in the field of nuclear physics and has no place in other contexts. It's not a synonym for *criticalness*.

Injecting jargon is just another technique that malescribes use to make sentences unclear and thereby compel their readers to take responsibility for discovering the intended meaning. Malescribes need to become more responsible, choosing words that are appropriate in meaning and appropriate to the intended audience.

> **HEALING TIP:**
>
> Use jargon sparingly and only when you're certain it will be understood.

Embracing Step 7

THE SEVENTH STEP TOWARD RECOVERY WILL FREE you from the need to leave readers guessing because of indefinite words and vague references.

Step 7: Stop writing unclear sentences.

In working through this step, you're deciding to give up writing techniques that are rooted in indifference. You're accepting the idea that the more care you exercise in your writing, the clearer and more complete it will be. So you're making a commitment to be responsible for providing the words and elaboration necessary for your sentences to make sense.

To eliminate unclear sentences, just follow this chapter's healing tips:

- When using a pronoun, make sure that its antecedent is obvious.
- Don't use *etc.* or any other uninformative word or phrase.
- Avoid using lazy words that merely express your approval or disapproval.
- Whenever you make a comparison, be sure to include some kind of reference.

- Whenever you use an acronym (or abbreviation), be sure to explain what it represents.
- Use jargon sparingly and only when you're certain it will be understood.

By the way, this might be a good time to make a searching and fearless moral inventory of yourself. If you find this exercise too painful, make a searching and fearless moral inventory of someone else.

Endnotes

1. We can't be sure whether the pronoun "he" refers to "husband" or "brother-in-law."
2. It's not clear what "etc." is meant to replace.
3. "Fine" and "nice" are weak and uninformative words.
4. "Too difficult" and "too busy" need to be elaborated upon to make sense.
5. The acronym *NCTE* isn't explained (it stands for the National Council of Teachers of English).
6. "Psychogenic" is a specialized word that will be unfamiliar to most readers.

STEP 8

STOP WRITING CARELESS SENTENCES

(by Overcoming Regret)

EACH OF US CARRIES A PERSONAL "IF ONLY" LIST that reminds us of our disappointments, missed opportunities, and frustrations. If you're a malescribe, yours might include some of the following:

- If only I'd paid attention in English class.
- If only my grades had been better.
- If only my parents had taken the time to understand my poetry.
- If only I'd won that essay contest.
- If only I'd had better teachers.

Regret about early writing-related events can motivate adult malescribes to make poor choices when constructing sentences. Let's learn a little about this maladaptive emotional response.

The Nature of Regret

AS CHILDREN, WE FELT PAIN AND UNHAPPINESS whenever we realized things hadn't gone the way we wanted. And as our egos took more and more insults, we began developing defense mechanisms. One such mechanism was the "if only" list. It allowed us to justify our *current* attitudes and capabilities by pointing to the harmful effects of *past* experiences. It allowed us to believe that we were simply innocent victims of our past.

As we matured, most of us—including malescribes—learned to live in the present and to try to bring about satisfying personal and professional lives. But when writing, malescribes are different from the rest of us because they are immobilized by regret. Instead of focusing on the present writing moment, they let past experiences limit their ability to communicate well. Regret gives malescribes an excuse for their inadequate verbal awareness. By shifting the responsibility for their woeful writing to the past, they create an excuse for *today's* absentminded decisions.

Your inner child-writer still wants to hold on to the comfort of blaming others and avoiding responsibility. So the way adult malescribes subconsciously express regret is by being nonchalant in choosing and arranging words. In other words, they write **careless sentences.** By writing carelessly, malescribes *appear* to be making unintentional mistakes. But, in fact, those mistakes are all about *control.* Malescribes subconsciously are trying to force their readers to put forth extra effort to make sense out of poorly written sentences.

Let's look at some of the techniques malescribes use to keep themselves blameless for the frustration that their sentences will inevitably create.

Being Inattentive to Word Order

"When I was a kid, I was forced to do my homework at a small table that was built by my father with wobbly legs. No wonder I can't write well!"[1]

MALESCRIBES, WRITING INTUITIVELY, OFTEN WILL place words haphazardly in a sentence. The result can be confusing, misleading, or distracting.

Here's an example:

• Mrs. Hargrove broke her hip after falling again.

Is the writer saying that Mrs. Hargrove fell again (and broke her hip for the first time) or that she broke her hip again (after falling)? There's no way to decide because of the careless word order.

Now let's look at an example where an adverb is placed carelessly:

- The father-to-be who was pacing frantically asked the nurse for a sedative.

Was the father-to-be *pacing frantically*, or did he *frantically ask* for a sedative? Because of the thoughtless placement of the adverb *frantically*, we can't be sure how it was intended to function in this sentence.

Careless word order can produce not only confusion but unintended humor as well, as in this sentence:

- The tape deck was designed by our engineer with three heads.

Malescribes spend much of their time and effort regretting past writing experiences and missed opportunities. So they are unable to do *in the present* what is needed to communicate clearly. And one of those things is to arrange words in the best possible way.

Confusing Similar Words

"Except for grammar and punctuation, my principle difficulty lies in diction."[2]

THE ENGLISH LANGUAGE IS FULL OF WORD PAIRS that are similar in pronunciation or appearance. For example, *principal* and *principle* sound alike but have different meanings.

Healthy writers know the importance of choosing the proper word. But malescribes, seeing writing through their "regret filter," believe that it's enough just to "get it close." This blasé attitude reflects a lack of awareness of the importance of present writing-moment choices. Malescribes fail to see that their carelessness can lead to misunderstanding and confusion.

Below is a list of some of the most commonly confused words, along with sentences that clarify their usage. Do you see any that have given you trouble?

accept/except
- I don't accept charity except when I really need it.

affect/effect
- Bill bribed the judges to affect the outcome of the contest; however, the effect was minimal.

bad/badly
- Jason feels bad whenever he writes badly.

between/among
- Helga had to decide between two skirts; Gunther had to decide among three shirts.

bi-/semi-
- The biannual issues come out in January and July, and the semiannual issues come out in odd-numbered years.

can/may
- I know that you can drive, but you may not drive on this trip.

capital/capitol
- In Raleigh, the capital city, the legislature has always met in the capitol building.

complement/compliment

- Whenever Ally's blouse complements her skirt, I compliment her on her good taste.

continuous/continual

- Judy finally realized that the continuous flow of cool air into the office was responsible for her continual sneezing.

discreet/discrete

- The detective was discreet in disclosing to Mrs. Fowler four discrete occurrences of her husband's infidelity.

eminent/imminent

- The staff was alerted because the arrival of the eminent statesman was imminent.

further/farther

- After further discussion, we decided that we would jog farther than we usually do.

less/fewer

- The second movie was less entertaining than the first, and fewer than twenty people remained to watch it.

imply/infer
- I sincerely implied that my readers were intelligent, but they inferred that I was being sarcastic.

into/in
- When we walked into the house, we found the cat sleeping in the living room.

ensure/insure
- To ensure that you don't experience catastrophic losses, insure your property.

laid/lay
- Around midafternoon I laid down my book, and then I lay down for a nap.

principal/principle
- In his speech to the school, the principal emphasized that students should follow their principles.

sit/set
- When I sit down to work, I have to set my knitting aside.

shoot/chute
- If you shoot a revolver inside a laundry chute, you'll create a deafening noise.

stationery/stationary

- Despite the earthquake, the stationery on the store's shelves remained stationary.

Malescribes can speed their recovery by reviewing this list every day for two weeks.

HEALING TIP:

Stay alert to words that are easily confused.

Using Nonparallel Terms

"I've often wondered, are women and guys equally likely to become malescribes?"[3]

HEALTHY WRITERS KNOW THAT SENTENCE ELEMENTS that have similar functions should be expressed with *parallel terms* (for example, the parallel term for *women* is *men*). This technique makes it easy for readers to recognize how various sentence elements are related.

But malescribes don't see the importance of providing these helpful cues. So they often fail to use parallel terms, thereby missing an opportunity to provide important information that can aid comprehension.

Let's look at five ways malescribes introduce faulty parallelism into their sentences.

1. *With nouns:*

- Both Republicans and liberals were in favor of the new budget.

Here, the parallel term for *Republicans* would be *Democrats* (because both identify members of a political party).

2. *With verbs:*

- The newlyweds decided to build a house rather than buying one.

In this sentence the related actions should be parallel:

- The newlyweds decided to build a house rather than buy one.

3. *With voice:*

- After I prepared the spaghetti, it was served by me to the whole family.

Because the first part of this sentence is in the active voice, the second part should be, too:

- After I prepared the spaghetti, I served it to the whole family.

4. *With wordy phrases:*

- This conference is for writers and people who read.

In this example, the parallel term for *writers* would be *readers,* not *people who read:*

- This conference is for writers and readers.

5. *In a series:*

- Don and Caroline enjoyed hiking, dancing, and to drive in the mountains.

Here the activities should be parallel:

- Don and Caroline enjoyed hiking, dancing, and driving in the mountains.

Using a nonparallel construction can make compre-hension more difficult, and it can sometimes imply a judgment or bias that many readers will notice. So male-scribes should be on the lookout for faulty parallelism in their writing.

HEALING TIP:

Express similar ideas in similar ways to help readers understand your point.

Overlooking the Sounds of Words

"Sometimes the reaction of readers to my writing really riles me."[4]

WORDS ON A PAGE OBVIOUSLY HAVE A *GRAPHICAL*, or visual, component. But written words also have a strong *phonological*, or sound based, component. Although silent readers don't verbalize what they read, the words are, in a sense, heard internally. And those internal sounds can occasionally become distracting.

Here's a sentence where the sounds of words come into play:

- Sherry's sixth session served to break her of her gambling habit.

The repetition of the "s" sound attracts attention and thus slows reading.

Although this technique can be effective in poetry (for emphasis) and in advertising (as a memory aid), it is out of place in most writing. Malescribes should become aware of the problem as they travel the path to recovery.

Ignoring Unintended Connotations

"I don't think I could have faced my writing problems without my husband's support. He's been a stone during this ordeal."[5]

WORDS HAVE *DENOTATIONS* (THEIR ACTUAL MEAN-ings) and *connotations* (their implied meanings). Often words that have similar denotations connote different ideas. For example, *stone* and *rock* are synonyms, but only *rock* suggests the positive qualities of steadiness and reliability.

Let's look at a few examples where the connotations of words have been overlooked:

- A laborer in the Philosophy Department received the university's Outstanding Teacher Award.
- The car crash that killed my daughter was terrific.
- Debbie was a handsome teenage girl.
- We watched two spry five year olds playing in the surf.

Consider the words *laborer, terrific, handsome,* and *spry* in these four examples. Their denotations make them functionally correct, but they seem inappropriate because they are used almost exclusively in other contexts. *Laborer* is usually associated with blue-collar jobs, *terrific* with a positive event, *handsome* with men, and *spry* with the elderly.

You can see that just because words share an element of meaning doesn't mean they can be used interchangeably. Using a word outside its usual context can distract readers and convey an unintended meaning. So it's important to pay attention to what words *suggest* and how they typically are used.

Relying on Spell Checkers

"I rely or my computer's spell checker. So if my writing isn't clear, its not my fault!"[6]

ONE OF THE MORE POPULAR MYTHS IN THE WRITING world is that spell checkers can make bad writing look good. But what malescribes fail to grasp is that spell checkers don't understand a writer's intentions.

Let's look at two sentences that illustrate this point:

- In good design, from follows function.
- Ron and Evelyn always give there children the best of everything.

If you type *from* when you mean *form* or *there* when you mean *their,* the errors won't be caught by a spell checker. Your readers will be forced to become editors to figure out what you meant.

Furthermore, spell checkers won't catch punctuation

mistakes. So if you write *its* when you meant *it's,* the mistake won't be noticed because *its* is a legitimate word.

Although technology is useful, it's not responsible for the content and clarity of your writing. If you rely on it to make your writing better, you might actually be communicating *less* effectively in print. Becoming a healthy writer involves becoming accountable for the content of your sentences.

HEALING TIP:

After using a spell checker, proofread your writing carefully.

Embracing Step 8

THE EIGHTH STEP TOWARD RECOVERY WILL FREE YOU from the need to make absentminded choices about words and the way they are arranged.

Step 8: Stop writing careless sentences.

By working through this step, you're deciding that you no longer will use regret to justify poor writing. You're declaring that you now will focus on the present writing moment and accept responsibility for the clarity of your words. Beginning today, your writing will no longer be about manipulating people into guessing at your intended meaning.

To eliminate careless sentences, remember this chapter's healing tips:

- Arrange words carefully to avoid misunderstanding.
- Stay alert to words that are easily confused.
- Express similar ideas in similar ways to help readers understand your point.
- Beware of the sounds of the words you choose.
- Consider the connotations of the words you use.
- After using a spell checker, proofread your writing carefully.

Endnotes

1. "With wobbly legs" should follow "a small table."
2. "Principle" should be "principal."
3. The parallel word for "women" is "men."
4. The many "r" sounds are distracting.
5. "Stone" doesn't suggest the same positive quality that "rock" would in this context.
6. "Or" should be "on." "Its" should be "it's."

STEP 9

STOP WRITING
UNPERSUASIVE SENTENCES

(by Overcoming Doubt)

"*WILL ANYBODY CARE WHAT I HAVE TO SAY? DO MY ideas count?*" This type of negative self-talk is one way malescribes express and reinforce *doubt* about the value of their own ideas, judgments, and concerns. Instead of focusing on the present writing-moment, they often waste time and energy questioning their own worth and the validity of their thoughts.

Doubt, like the other emotions we've examined, has a payoff: it gives malescribes an excuse for their underdeveloped verbal skills. Let's learn a little more about this dysfunctional writing habit.

Understanding Doubt

DURING YOUR FIRST YEARS, YOUR PARENTS MADE ALL of your decisions for you. They decided what you would eat, what you would wear, and where you would go. But after a while you began trying to make some decisions yourself. Unfortunately, you quickly found out that your choices often clashed with what others felt were the "proper" choices.

The message you internalized was that your own choices were likely wrong. You began to understand that it was best to check with an adult before going ahead with any decision, lest you be overruled. So your self-esteem suffered. You learned not to trust yourself, but to look to others for validation of your ideas.

Today, your frustrated inner child-writer still feels inadequate. It wonders about the value of its feelings and choices. And the way adult malescribes subconsciously express that doubt is by writing tentatively, thereby failing to impress, convince, or motivate their readers. In other words, they write **unpersuasive sentences.**

Let's look at some of the self-defeating techniques that malescribes use to avoid having their choices challenged and overruled by their readers.

Ignoring the Reader's Perspective

"Although this recovery program is difficult, time-consuming, and emotionally draining, it's probably worthwhile."[1]

A PRINTED MESSAGE HAS TWO IMPORTANT ASPECTS: *content* and *tone*. The *content* is the literal message that is presented explicitly, whereas the *tone* is the subjective quality of the message that is presented implicitly. Let's see how these two aspects work together to affect the way people respond to a sentence.

Compare the following two sentences:

- Our low prices mean now is the time for you to make that decision to buy a new stereo.
- Let us show you how you can save money and enjoy your new stereo right away.

Although the two sentences have similar content, the tone differs. In the first sentence, we learn that we have to *decide* and *buy*. But in the second, we learn that we can *save* and *enjoy*. Which would *you* rather do? It's obvious that tone is a subtle but important factor in the way people initially react to what they read.

In general, words that suggest burden, discomfort, or

responsibility for readers will repel. But words that suggest gratification, improvement, or advantage will usually attract. When healthy writers try to persuade, they always take into account the way their audience will feel when reading their words. They understand that it's *their* responsibility to make it easy for people to become interested and attentive.

But malescribes, seeing the writing process through their "doubt filter," wonder about their ability to shape a sentence for best effect. Because they subconsciously fear being contradicted, they lower their expectations. They naively expect their readers to ignore the tone of a message and focus just on its content.

How will people feel when they read your message? Why will they be motivated to keep reading? Will they see that your ideas are meaningful to them? If you aren't sure of the answers to these questions, you probably won't be persuasive.

HEALING TIP:

To attract and hold readers, consider their points of view and make your message personally relevant to them.

Focusing on Features

"I recommend this twelve-step program because of its logical structure, thoroughness, and practical illustrations."[2]

MOST THINGS CAN BE DESCRIBED IN TERMS OF *FEATURES* and *benefits*. What's the difference? A *feature* is a characteristic. A *benefit* is a positive effect produced by a feature. Compare each feature listed below with its benefit:

Feature	Benefit
well written	easy to read
ergonomically designed	comfortable to use
inexpensive	affordable

As you can see, features answer the question "What is it?" and give an idea of *quality*. But benefits answer the question "What does it mean to *me?*" and give an idea of *value*.

In the following two sentences, notice the difference in focus:

- Acme locks are made from the best materials, come with a two-year warranty, and can be professionally installed.

- You and your family deserve peace of mind, and you'll have it when Acme locks are protecting your home.

People don't need well-built locks—they need the security that those locks provide. Features are impersonal, whereas benefits are personal and therefore meaningful to readers.

> **HEALING TIP:**
>
> When trying to convince readers of the value of something, focus on its benefits instead of its features.

Failing to Encourage Agreement or Action

"I think it's important for malescribes to get help, and I hope people agree with me."[3]

ALTHOUGH YOU CAN'T *FORCE* READERS TO THINK OR do anything, you can make it easier for them to be swayed. By consciously guiding and encouraging your readers, you make it more likely that your writing will convince and motivate.

One way to encourage readers is to answer basic questions such as *how? when?* and *where?* (questions that malescribes assume readers will answer for themselves). For example, let's say you want people in your community to recycle. Compare these two approaches to the problem:

- Be kind to the environment: take all recyclable materials to the nearest collection bins in your neighborhood.
- Be kind to the environment: recycle your aluminum cans, newspapers, and cardboard by bringing them to the bins at Westgate Mall.

The first sentence merely states the writer's desire. But the second helps readers by explicitly stating *how* to agree and comply. It is more likely to get a response because it encourages readers with specific guidelines.

Another way to encourage readers is to use words that suggest activity, movement, or urgency. Here are a few examples:

call
do
go
immediately

limited time
now
order
save
see
soon
switch
today
visit
write

Action words *encourage* rather than merely suggest. They give the impression that *doing* something might be to the reader's advantage. And healthy writers know that it's *their* job to make that idea clear to readers.

HEALING TIP:

Use specific motivational language that encourages readers to agree and respond.

Failing to Make Information Memorable

"There are many reasons to improve your writing skills, so I think you should do it."[4]

IF PEOPLE CAN'T REMEMBER WHAT YOU'VE WRITTEN, they certainly aren't going to be influenced by it. The problem you face is that human memory has limitations: information might be remembered incorrectly or incompletely, recalled with difficulty, or forgotten altogether. So writers can benefit from learning some simple techniques that help people remember the information they read.

The most obvious way to aid memory is to *provide adequate information* for making your point. If you present vague or incomplete ideas, your readers won't have anything worthwhile to remember. It's important, however, not to overload your readers with excessive details. If readers are inundated with facts and figures, they might have trouble isolating your main point.

Mnemonics, or memory techniques, are also useful. One technique is to associate something new with something already known. Compare the following two sentences and you'll see how effective association can be:

- Saturday's "Defeat Malescribism" march will begin at 1500 Markham Street at noon.

- Saturday's "Defeat Malescribism" march will begin at 1500 Markham Street (next to Burger King) at noon.

The second version is much more effective because it links an address, which is just a number, with a familiar and easily recognizable landmark.

Another technique that aids memory is to create a vivid mental image to make a point. Here's an example:

- Thanks to our mayor's policies, our city's economy has changed from a well-tuned racer to a sputtering jalopy.

In this sentence, the writer links two economic states with two easy-to-visualize cars that have different capabilities. And when information is "processed" both verbally and visually, it is easier to remember.

In addition to association and imagery, writers can also make use of *repetition, rhyme,* and *humor* to create a more memorable message. The most appropriate technique in a given situation will be determined by the audience, the type of message, and your goals.

Malescribes need to realize that they have the power to manipulate a sentence so that it achieves its goal. They can shape it and embellish it so that the message becomes easier to remember.

Using Faulty Reasoning

"Everyone has trouble writing, so there's really no point in trying to improve my verbal skills."[5]

SOME PIECES OF WRITING NEED TO BE PARTICULARLY persuasive, presenting an argument based on facts or conditions. For example, you might write a letter to an editor to criticize a proposed highway project. Or you might write a memo at work to request new software. Or you might write a newsletter article enlisting support for a cause or concern. Will you be persuasive? Will readers find your arguments convincing? You can increase the chances of success by avoiding the four traps explained below.

1. *Generalization:* Extending an assertion beyond what is justifiable.

Here are a few examples:

- Men don't know how to express their feelings.
- If grade inflation is a problem at State College, I'm sure it's a problem at all colleges.
- Rich people don't care about anyone but themselves.
- Anyone with a criminal record is a threat to society.

In each example the contention is that similar things must share whatever characteristic the writer happens to mention. But because no support or proof is offered, the arguments are unconvincing.

2. *False cause and effect:* Asserting that one thing caused another because of the order in which they occurred.

- Average SAT scores dropped soon after our governor took office, so we need to elect a new pro-education leader for our state.

Here it is implied that the governor is responsible for the lower SAT scores simply because his election preceded the drop. This type of error stems from overlooking (intentionally or not) the existence of numerous other variables that may have contributed to the change.

3. *Circular reasoning:* Using a statement as its own explanation.

- Trucks and SUVs cause problems on the road because they create difficulties for other drivers.

Here trucks and SUVs are said to *cause problems* because they *create difficulties*. So the writer has merely stated the opinion in two different ways and has offered no reasons for holding it.

4. *Non sequitur (Latin for "it does not follow"):* Making an unwarranted connection between two ideas or events.

- We don't know when interest rates will be this low again, so now is the time to consider refinancing.

In this example the premise is really "Interest rates might go up or down or stay the same." So there's no basis for recommending *any* particular course of action. Here are a few other examples:

- With a Harvard degree, Jack will have no trouble finding a good job.

- Amanda is a talented writer, so I know she will be a great writing teacher.
- Just look at the increase in crime! We need more gun laws.

In each case a fact or opinion is used as the basis for a questionable conclusion.

Faulty reasoning can weaken your writing and cause readers to be inattentive, unimpressed, or unconvinced. Recovering malescribes need to realize that a persuasive argument must be built on a solid foundation.

> **HEALING TIP:**
>
> Make sure your conclusions are justifiable and based on facts and clear thinking.

Omitting Critical Information

"They say that writing skill isn't all that important in the digital age, so the value of this twelve-step program is minimal."[6]

AS CHILDREN WE OFTEN ANSWERED THE QUESTION "Why?" by saying, "Because." Adult malescribes often use the same approach when attempting to write persuasively. They feel that merely stating their opinion is enough to convince their readers. It's as if they expect others to read their minds and to share their assumptions and biases.

NOW LET'S LOOK AT SOME OF THE MISGUIDED TECHniques that malescribes resort to in hope of avoiding the work of explaining their opinions.

1. *Questionable authority:* Attempting to add weight to an opinion by referring to unnamed experts.

- We must have bilingual education because leading educators agree that it's the wisest course.

Who are these educators, why are they qualified, and what, exactly, did they say? The writer doesn't give enough information to make the argument convincing.

2. *Imprecise terms:* Including words that have no clear meaning.

- The school's new afternoon programs are of little value, and therefore should be discontinued.

Of little value to whom? Without more elaboration, readers are unlikely to be swayed toward this writer's position.

3. *Personal attack:* Questioning the right of a person to have an opinion instead of examining the validity of that opinion.

• Residents of Manhattan have no right to criticize the decisions of midwestern farmers.

Why not? If there is a reason, the writer has failed to present it and therefore has missed a chance to add some credibility to the statement.

4. *Oversimplification:* Implying that there are only two sides to an issue—yours and the wrong one.

• Nobody who cares about America would drive a foreign car.

Why wouldn't they? And can "caring about America" really be defined so simply? This writer has merely stated a *belief* that two activities are incompatible without providing any logical support.

* * *

ALL OF THESE TECHNIQUES DIVERT ATTENTION AWAY from the real issue: Why do you hold a particular opinion, and why should anyone agree with you? In the foregoing examples, critical information that might have made the statements persuasive is unstated. It's left to the reader to guess at the missing elements. Such sentences can have little persuasive power.

> **HEALING TIP:**
>
> When expressing an opinion, make sure you state your case *explicitly* and give valid reasons for supporting it.

Embracing Step 9

THE NINTH STEP TOWARD RECOVERY WILL FREE YOU from the need to avoid assertive, confident expression.

Step 9: Stop writing unpersuasive sentences.

In working through this step, you're declaring your freedom from the oppressive power of doubt. You're deciding to empower yourself with a sense of self-worth and write with confidence and optimism. And you're saying that you no longer will naively expect your readers to motivate and convince themselves for your benefit.

To eliminate unpersuasive sentences from your writing, remember this chapter's healing tips:

- To attract and hold readers, consider their points of view and make your message personally relevant to them.
- When trying to convince readers of the value of something, focus on its benefits instead of its features.
- Use specific motivational language that encourages readers to agree and respond.
- When appropriate, help readers remember your message by using association, imagery, repetition, rhyme, or humor.
- Make sure your conclusions are justifiable and based on facts and clear thinking.
- When expressing an opinion, make sure you state your case *explicitly* and give valid reasons for supporting it.

By the way, if you feel the need to call on a higher power, as you perceive it, to remove your verbal shortcomings, please do so. (No, an e-mail is not appropriate.)

Endnotes

1. The sentence creates a negative tone and fails to motivate the reader.

2. It would be more persuasive to mention the benefits of the program.

3. "I hope people agree with me" isn't confident or persuasive.

4. No specific reasons are offered for improving your writing skills.

5. "Everyone has trouble writing" is an unsubstantiated generalization.

6. We don't know who "they" are, and we don't know to whom the program is of minimal value.

STEP 10

STOP WRITING
INCONGRUOUS SENTENCES

(by Overcoming Anger)

SO FAR, WE'VE SEEN HOW BAD WRITING SATISFIES the unhealthy needs for resistance, approval, and control. Now, in the final three steps of the recovery program, we'll examine the need for *defiance*. We'll see how anger, rebelliousness, and stubbornness—all forms of defiance—motivate malescribes to make bad choices as they write.

Defiance is a way of convincing ourselves that we are right, powerful, and in control. It is a way of blaming others and shifting responsibility. And it gives us an excuse for not learning and growing.

We'll start with *anger*. And we'll see how this destructive emotion can lead malescribes to make grammatical "mistakes" that really are indirect attempts to confront and challenge their readers.

Understanding Anger

ANGER IS A KNEE-JERK RESPONSE TO A PERCEIVED threat. When we think that something we value might be taken away, we react defensively. As children, we couldn't deal with threats to our self-centered lifestyle intellectually or physically—we simply didn't have that capability. But we could react emotionally, by crying and yelling. In doing so we created discomfort for our parents.

As we matured, we gradually learned to tolerate the system. And although we became more deferential toward adults, we still needed to protect ourselves when we felt emotionally threatened. So we developed less direct ways of expressing anger: we pouted, fumed, or became uncooperative. Thus we avoided the unpleasant feelings that a direct confrontation would have aroused.

Most of us overcame these passive-aggressive tendencies because we realized that they were counterproductive in the adult world. Over and over we restrained our instinctive need to lash out and defend our fragile egos. And in the process, without knowing it, we left behind many unresolved conflicts that lodged themselves in the dark corners of our subconscious minds.

Your frustrated inner child-writer still feels the pressure from early emotional threats that were never adequately deflected. And it needs to fight back in some way—but it can't. So adult malescribes subconsciously express that anger and defiance by filling their writing with conflicting and inharmonious elements that hinder comprehension. In other words, they write **incongruous sentences.**

Let's take a look at some techniques malescribes use to vent their anger and thereby cause discomfort for their readers.

Writing Sentence Fragments

"I really didn't like my ninth-grade English teacher. With her smug look and stupid assignments."[1]

EVERY SENTENCE HAS TWO ESSENTIAL ELEMENTS: *subject* and *verb*. The *subject* acts or is acted upon, and the *verb** describes the action. Together, subject and verb create a complete thought.

In a sentence fragment, either the subject or the verb is missing. The thought expressed is incomplete, leaving room for misinterpretation.

Here's an example of a sentence fragment:

---

*Predicate is the precise word for a verb or verb phrase and the words that complete or modify it.

- I like reminiscing about my trip to Europe. Riding trains, eating unusual food, taking photos.

You can see that the fragment ("Riding trains . . .") lacks a verb and doesn't present a fully formed idea. A critical element has been withheld, and readers are left with the task of guessing what it is.

Sentence fragments are, in some cases, acceptable. For example, they can be used effectively to present dialogue, emphasize a point, or answer a question, as illustrated here:

- "Where have you been? At the library?"
- Bill won a full scholarship. What an opportunity!
- How did I succeed? With persistence, of course.

In each of these examples, the complete sentence creates a context into which the fragment fits. So confusion is unlikely.

Using Dangling Modifiers

"Working through this twelve-step program, my grammar has improved." [2]

A MODIFYING PHRASE PROVIDES INFORMATION ABOUT the subject of a sentence, as shown here:

- Worried about final exams, Maggie tossed and turned all night.

In this example, the initial phrase clearly modifies, or describes, the subject *(Maggie),* which is included in the second part of the sentence.

Healthy writers always make sure the word that's being modified is, in fact, the true subject of the sentence. But malescribes, seeing writing through their "anger filter," often will "forget" to make clear exactly what the subject is. And the result can be a *dangling modifier*—a phrase that incorrectly modifies a word that isn't the subject. When a modifier dangles, it creates an incongruous sentence.

Let's look at two types of modifying phrases that frequently are left to dangle by malescribes.

One type of dangling modifier involves verbs ending in *-ing* (called *present participles*). Here's an example:

- Searching the car, my wallet was soon found.

Here the modifying phrase *searching the car* appears to modify *my wallet,* which is absurd. Because *I* was the one doing the searching, *I* should be the subject of the sentence. A small change can eliminate the problem:

- Searching the car, I soon found my wallet.

The sentence now makes sense. The participial phrase no longer dangles because it modifies the subject that appears in the second part of the sentence.

Here are a few other examples of dangling participles:

- Turning on the light, the surprise party began.
- Entering the museum, the dinosaur skeleton attracted everyone's attention.
- Driving to Grandma's house, our two year old always dozes off.

In each example, notice that the modifying phrase lacks a subject. And because the subject is also missing in the second part of the sentence, incongruity occurs.

Another type of dangling modifier involves *infinitive* phrases (*to* followed by a verb). Here's an example:

- To become a teacher, a college degree is needed.

The phrase *to become a teacher* needs to modify something, and here, *college degree* is the only thing available. Since that idea makes no sense, the sentence needs to be revised:

- To become a teacher, you will need a college degree.

In this version, the incongruity has been removed. The first phrase now correctly modifies the true subject of the sentence *(you)*.

HEALING TIP:

When using a participial or infinitive phrase, make sure it modifies the true subject of the sentence.

Misusing Pronouns

"If someone is a malescribe, will they always write poorly?"[3]

PRONOUNS, SUCH AS *HIM, HERS,* AND *THEY,* TAKE the place of nouns and allow us to communicate concisely. But a pronoun makes sense only if it refers unambiguously to a particular noun (called the *antecedent*).

Standard English demands that singular pronouns refer to singular nouns, and that plural pronouns refer to plural nouns. In other words, a pronoun must *agree* (or be compatible) with its antecedent in *number.* When malescribes fail to follow the rule, they create *incongruous sentences.*

Notice the disagreement in the following sentence:

- When a person writes novels, they should use original plots.

In this example, the careless use of *they* to refer to *person* creates a moment of confusion. The pronoun *(they)* is plural, but its antecedent *(person)* is singular.

To eliminate the disagreement, we have several options. One is to use the traditional method where the pronoun *he* is used inclusively:

- When a person writes novels, he should use original plots.

In this version, pronoun and antecedent agree. And because readers understand that both men and women write novels (and because *person* doesn't exclude anyone), the meaning of the sentence is clear.

Another option is to use the *he or she* construction:

- When a person writes novels, he or she should use original plots.

Once again pronoun and antecedent agree because they are both singular. There is no incongruity.

Neither of these options will satisfy all readers. Some will complain that inclusive use of *he* is old-fashioned, and some will complain that continual use of *he or she* is clumsy and distracting. Fortunately, we have two other ways to ensure agreement between noun and pronoun.

One approach is to use a plural subject and pronoun, as shown here:

- When people write novels, they should use original plots.

Here the pronoun *they* agrees in number with the antecedent *people*.

Another approach is simply to eliminate the need for an antecedent by using an introductory modifying phrase, as shown here:

- When writing novels, you should use original plots.

Here, no antecedent is needed, so there's no potential disagreement.

Pronouns help us to write economically and smoothly. But when they disagree with their antecedents, they create an incongruous image that can cause readers to hesitate, reread, and question your true meaning.

HEALING TIP:

Make sure pronouns agree with their antecedents in number.

Creating Subject/Verb Disagreement

"Neither my diction nor my syntax have ever been better!" [4]

WE JUST LEARNED HOW IMPORTANT IT IS TO HAVE agreement between pronouns and their antecedents. Similarly, agreement is important for subjects and verbs. The rule is simple: a singular subject requires a singular verb, and a plural subject requires a plural verb. The key to success is to identify the subject of each sentence.

Let's look at four potential sources of confusion when it comes to creating agreement between subjects and verbs.

1. *Compound subjects*

If the subject of a sentence consists of more than one noun, a plural verb should be used, as shown here:

• Jogging and dieting help me stay fit.

The conjunction *and* creates a compound subject *(jogging and dieting),* and a plural verb *(help)* is required.

An exception occurs if a compound subject represents an entity, such as a team or a company.

• Smith and Blake has agreed to handle the lawsuit.

Here *Smith and Blake* is the name of a (single) law firm, and therefore it functions as a singular subject and requires a singular verb.

2. *Modifying phrases*

A phrase that modifies a subject does not become part of the subject. Take a look at a sentence that includes a modifying phrase:

- Kim, along with many of her friends, was late for class.

Here, *along with* is not a conjunction (like *and*) and does not create a compound subject. The phrase merely modifies the subject *(Kim)*. So the subject is singular, and a singular verb *(was)* is required.

Other phrases that can modify a subject in this way are *accompanied by, in addition to,* and *as well as.*

3. *Troublesome words*

The words *each, any,* and *either* take a singular verb, as shown in the examples below:

- Each of the committee members was asked about the decision.
- Any of those students is capable of great success.
- Either the president or the CEO is responsible.

In each case a singular verb is needed because the word *one* is implied (for example, *any* really suggests *anyone*).

With the word *either,* an exception applies when the subject is compound and consists of a singular noun and a plural noun, as seen here:

- Either the coach or the team members were responsible.

Because the verb is closer to the plural noun *(members),* a plural verb is appropriate.

4. *"Flexible" plural nouns*

Just because the subject of a sentence *contains* a plural noun doesn't mean we can assume that the subject itself is plural. Compare the following two correctly written sentences:

- Five quarters are in my hand.
- Five dollars is not a lot of money.

You can see that when a plural noun represents items that are to be considered *individually (five quarters),* a plural verb is needed. But when a plural noun represents items that are to be considered *collectively (five dollars),* a singular verb is needed. It's important to consider how the subject is used in the sentence before deciding on the verb.

Using Tense Inconsistently

"For years, I wrote unimaginatively and punctuated carelessly. But one day, I look in the mirror and see a malescribe! I realized it was time to act."[5]

ONE OF THE RESPONSIBILITIES OF A HEALTHY WRITER is to convey a clear sense of how sentence elements relate to one another over time. This effect is achieved with consistent use of verb tense.

In the following sentence, notice the careless switching of verb tenses:

- The article in the *Times* makes a good point. It said that anyone who invested in stocks has to be patient. And if they are, their money grew.

In this example the variety of verb tenses creates an unclear time sequence. Consistency can make the sentence clearer, as shown here:

- The article in the *Times* makes a good point. It says that anyone who invests in stocks has to be patient. And if they are, their money will grow.

Inattention to verb tense can lead to *incongruous sentences* that leave readers wondering what you're really trying to say. So be sure to establish a logical sense of time when you write.

> **HEALING TIP:**
>
> Don't switch verb tense without a good reason.

Mixing and Mangling Metaphors

"I finally started this twelve-step program because I felt it was time to step up to the plate and take the bull by the horns."[6]

METAPHORS ARE NONLITERAL PHRASES THAT MAKE writing more vivid and interesting. They can be used to suggest images and to make subtle (or obvious) comparisons. But in the hands of malescribes, they often are used to create incongruity.

One mistake involves misusing a familiar metaphor, as illustrated in these two sentences:

- All semester, Vicky kept her ear to the grind-stone.
- We'll tackle that bridge when we come to it.

In each example, parts of two unrelated metaphors are combined to create one that will cause most readers to do a mental double take.

Extending a metaphor is another mistake malescribes often make, as shown here:

- Jerry thought of his life as a single long paragraph, punctuated at times intuitively and at times according to the rules of grammar, showing evidence of continual editing and proofreading by friends and others, and set in a variety of typefaces.

Here the writer dilutes the metaphor with excessive detail.

Although metaphors are not intended to be taken literally, their literal meanings can emerge occasionally and create a problem. Take the following sentence:

- The protesters took a stand by sitting in front of the courthouse door.

Here the literal meaning of *took a stand* comes to mind because of the word *sitting*. We get an incongruous image of people who are standing and sitting simultaneously!

Figurative language can make writing more engaging and more memorable. But if it suggests incompatible or unlikely images, it can become a distraction to readers.

HEALING TIP:

Enliven your writing with metaphors—but use them correctly and with restraint.

Embracing Step 10

THE TENTH STEP TOWARD RECOVERY WILL FREE YOU from the need to fill your writing with conflicting and incompatible words and phrases.

Step 10: Stop writing incongruous sentences.

In working through this step, you're making the decision to eliminate discordant, inconsistent elements from your writing. In doing so you are empowering yourself to rise above your anger at others—and at yourself.

To eliminate incongruous sentences, follow the healing tips in this chapter:

- To express a complete thought, include both a subject and a verb in every sentence.
- When using a participial or infinitive phrase, make sure it modifies the true subject of the sentence.
- Make sure pronouns agree with their antecedents in number.
- Use a singular verb with a singular subject, and a plural verb with a plural subject.
- Don't switch verb tense without a good reason.
- Enliven your writing with metaphors—but use them correctly and with restraint.

Endnotes

1. The second sentence is really a sentence fragment (it lacks both subject and predicate).
2. The initial modifying phrase demands that the subject of the second phrase be "I," not "my grammar."
3. "They" is a plural pronoun, but it incorrectly refers to the singular noun "someone."
4. "Have" should be "has."
5. The switch between past and present tenses is confusing.
6. Two incompatible metaphors are linked.

STOP WRITING
UNSTRUCTURED SENTENCES

(by Overcoming Rebelliousness)

IF YOU'RE LIKE MOST PEOPLE, YOU CAN UNDERSTAND
what is meant by the following string of letters:

- canyoureadthis

Although this "sentence" lacks the conventional and
expected structure, it can be understood. Readers are able
to impose patterns on the string of letters and organize it
so it makes sense. But you certainly wouldn't want to put
forth that kind of effort every time you read something.

Although malescribes might not go to such extremes,
they often do create sentences that are poorly organized.
By being inattentive to the *structure* of sentences, they
create the opportunity for misunderstanding. Their words
might be chosen carefully and spelled correctly, but they

don't necessarily work together as well as they should to convey the intended meaning. Malescribes, of course, naively assume that their readers will be willing to imagine the missing structure. Healthy writers know better.

In writing, structure is important for three reasons: First, it tells readers how words are related to one another in a sentence. Second, it directs attention to key words. Third, structure breaks a sentence into meaningful and manageable parts.

Malescribes probably understand *intellectually* the importance of sentence structure. But their subconscious *emotional* responses—including the need to defy their readers—usually win out. We've already seen how anger can motivate malescribes to make bad decisions. Now let's look at another aspect of defiance that is equally harmful to the writing process: *rebelliousness*.

Understanding Rebelliousness

THE NEED TO REBEL AGAINST PARENTS AND OTHER authority figures is part of human nature. It is a normal and healthy phase in the development of well-adjusted individuals. As children we all rebelled to challenge convention, question restrictions, and begin to establish ourselves as independent people.

As we gained confidence in "spreading our wings," we

became at times quarrelsome, indifferent, and uncooperative. And our parents became exasperated. They merely wanted the orderliness and predictability they had come to expect from us, but we needed to go our own way.

Eventually, the rebellion phase ran its course, and we began to see the value of a certain amount of conformity and cooperation. We came to realize that the rules weren't made just to vex us. But for some of us, the emotional issues behind the rebelliousness were never resolved.

Your inner child-writer still is looking for resolution to those issues. It feels the need to continue to rebel and to challenge those who make the rules. And the way adult malescribes subconsciously express this defiance is by neglecting to organize their thoughts effectively. They punctuate carelessly, arrange words intuitively, and ignore commonsense organizational principles. In other words, they write **unstructured sentences.**

Now let's take a look at some of the techniques malescribes use to introduce disorder into their writing and thereby frustrate their readers.

Omitting the Final Comma in a Series (the Serial Comma)

"Just how important is the proper use of dashes, semicolons and colons and commas?"[1]

HEALTHY WRITERS KNOW THAT COMMAS ARE RE-
quired to separate words in a series. Here is a sentence
that uses commas correctly:

• Juan enjoyed his dinner of steak, salad, and bread.

Here, the commas make it clear that *steak, salad,* and
bread are separate members of a single group (things that
Juan ate). The punctuation organizes the sentence in a
way that eliminates any potential misunderstanding.

But malescribes, relying on intuitive guidelines, often
omit the final (or serial) comma, as shown here:

• Juan enjoyed his dinner of steak, salad and bread.

Without the final comma, the sentence erroneously
gives the impression that *salad* and *bread* form a group,
and that *steak* isn't part of it. The incorrect punctuation
introduces some uncertainty about the way the three
words are related.

The problem lies in the fact that *and* is a conjunction—
it connects words. So when a reader encounters *and,* the
question becomes: How many words are being connected?
Healthy writers make it clear; malescribes don't.

The importance of the final comma is even more obvious when a compound element is included in a series.
Compare these two sentences:

- My favorite comedians are Laurel and Hardy, Chaplin, and Keaton.
- My favorite comedians are Laurel and Hardy, Chaplin and Keaton.

The first sentence correctly identifies three elements (the first one being compound). But in the second sentence, the omission of the final comma misleads us, at least momentarily, to think that *Chaplin and Keaton* should be considered a single element (as *Laurel and Hardy* is).

Is this emphasis on the final comma in a series arbitrary? No. Psychological research has shown that peripheral information (to the *right* of each momentary focus) creates *expectations* and thereby facilitates reading. The following partial sentence will clarify the point:

- After Sam met Judy, Kathy and Jan, his best friends . . .

At this point, we now expect that *Judy* will have a different function in the sentence than *Kathy and Jan*. If the sentence is grammatically correct, those expectations will be confirmed as we read further:

- After Sam met Judy, Kathy and Jan, his best friends, arrived.

As the absence of a serial comma led us to believe correctly, *Judy* is not part of the group consisting of *Kathy and Jan*.

But what if the writer had intended to say that the three women are members of a single group (people whom Sam met)? By carelessly omitting the final comma, the writer would have created expectations that would not be confirmed, as shown here:

- After Sam met Judy, Kathy and Jan, his best friends arrived.

Here, we are misled by the missing comma. There's no reason to expect that the three women are all part of the same group—and yet, surprisingly, they are. So the incorrect punctuation forces us to reread so we can make sense of the sentence.

Omitting a necessary comma can also create unintentional humor, as shown here:

- On my desk at work, I have pictures of my two little boys, Tina and Fluffy.

Commas identify relationships within a sentence. If you omit a necessary comma, you remove the structure that is just as important as the words themselves. And why would you do that if your goal is to communicate clearly?

HEALING TIP:

Never omit the final comma in a series.

Separating Subject and Verb

"My writing, which, of course, would benefit from better word selection, more careful punctuation, and attention to grammatical concerns such as split infinitives and dangling participles, isn't so bad."[2]

ENLIGHTENED WRITERS UNDERSTAND INSTINCTIVELY the organizational principle of *contiguity:* things are more likely to be perceived as related if they are close together. When these people create a sentence, they arrange words carefully, giving special attention to subject and verb. They know that these two elements are most important because they convey the main idea of each sentence.

But malescribes, seeing the writing process through

their "rebelliousness filter," are unable to keep the principle of contiguity in mind. They tend to write intuitively and show little concern for the positions of key words. It's a way of satisfying their need to challenge established ideas and resist conformity.

Here's an example of this misguided technique:

- In January the economy, after four straight quarters of lackluster and frustrating performance, especially in the automotive, telecommunications, and housing industries (excluding sales of existing homes), improved.

Here a simple idea *(the economy improved)* loses much of its impact because of the material that has been inserted between subject and verb. We have to make an extra effort to grasp the essence of the sentence.

The simplest solution would be to use two sentences to express the idea, as shown here:

- In January the economy improved after four straight quarters of lackluster and frustrating performance. Especially disappointing during the previous year were the automotive, telecommunications, and housing industries (excluding sales of existing homes).

In this version, the supporting material no longer interferes with the main point, and the sentence is more easily understood.

Recovering malescribes need to remember that reading takes place *over time*. As related words get separated further on a page, they also get separated further in time. Too much separation can weaken the connection, making comprehension more difficult.

HEALING TIP:

Keep the subject and verb of a sentence reasonably close together.

Splitting Infinitives

"Is it okay to boldly state my opinions when I write?"[3]

WE JUST LEARNED HOW SEPARATING SUBJECT AND verb can make their relationship within a sentence less clear. Now let's look at another frequently used sentence element—the *infinitive*—that also presents the opportunity for making a structural mistake.

An infinitive is the form of a verb with *to*. For example, *to go, to swim,* and *to write* are infinitives. Because the two words of an infinitive create one idea, there's no reason to separate them. Yet that is exactly what malescribes often do.

Let's see what happens when you split an infinitive. Here's an example:

- Carol tried to vigorously swim against the powerful current.

There's no denying that the sentence does make sense. But the essential action here is "to swim"—so why insert a modifier between the two words? We easily can avoid splitting the infinitive by rewriting the sentence as shown here:

- Carol tried to swim vigorously against the powerful current.

In this version the adverb *vigorously* has been moved and the infinitive *to swim* remains intact.

Occasionally, you might create a sentence wherein a split infinitive would be needed to avoid confusion or unintended humor. Compare the following two sentences:

- Sheila's job was to alertly watch comatose patients.

- Sheila's job was to watch alertly comatose patients.

Although the first sentence contains a split infinitive, it is preferred because it avoids the odd-looking phrase *alertly comatose*.

Splitting an infinitive doesn't necessarily make a sentence unclear. But it *is* often a pointless exercise that separates two words that clearly belong together.

HEALING TIP:

Avoid splitting an infinitive unless you will create an awkward sentence.

Neglecting to Group Related Words

"My support system includes my pastor, Spot, Ted, my therapist, Jill, and Ralph." [4]

MALESCRIBES ARE ADEPT AT JUSTIFYING THEIR IN-difference to sentence structure. They complain that it's too much trouble and takes too much time to organize sentences correctly. But, in fact, most organizing techniques are simple and easy to apply. One such technique—grouping related words—can greatly improve a sentence. Recovering malescribes need to learn how to use it.

First, take a look at the following sentence:

- In October, rainfall was above normal in Oregon, Vermont, New Hampshire, Washington, New York, Montana, and Maine.

This unstructured sentence is clear—just not clear enough. The impression we get from it is that rainfall was above normal *in seven states.* But is that fact really all the sentence needs to convey?

Let's improve the sentence by rearranging the states into two groups:

- In October, rainfall was above normal in Oregon, Washington, and Montana, and also in Vermont, New Hampshire, New York, and Maine.

In this version, we easily grasp that rainfall was above normal *in two particular sections of the country.* So this sentence is more informative than the first because it *groups* related items. Its organization tells us exactly how the seven states relate to one another.

What if more clarity or emphasis is desired? The solution is simple: use *labels* that identify the groups:

- In October, rainfall was above normal in the northwestern states of Oregon, Washington, and Montana, and also in the northeastern states of Vermont, New Hampshire, New York, and Maine.

The labels *northwestern states* and *northeastern states* identify explicitly the two groups of states. The labels certainly aren't essential, but they do make comprehension effortless and complete.

HEALING TIP:

Help readers by grouping (and, if necessary, labeling) related items.

Overlooking the Value of Colons, Dashes, and Parentheses

"I understand how to use all punctuation marks except one; the colon."[5]

ONE ESSENTIAL ASPECT OF HEALTHY WRITING IS THE ability to emphasize key ideas. We sometimes need to be able to direct the reader's attention to particular words. Because most people read fairly rapidly, the way to direct their attention is to slow the reading process momentarily. And the best tools for this job are colons, dashes, and parentheses.

These three punctuation marks often are overlooked by malescribes, who typically think of punctuation as relatively unimportant. But as we'll see, creative use of colons, dashes, and parentheses can add variety and interest to sentences. Let's take a look at these simple but powerful structural elements.

A *colon* can create an abrupt pause and introduce a word or phrase that deserves special notice. If you compare the following two sentences, you will see the value of the colon:

- I realized then that my only option was to stay and fight.
- I realized then that I had only one option: stay and fight.

In the second sentence, the colon adds impact to the phrase *stay and fight*. The punctuation sets off the phrase from the rest of the sentence, suggesting that it might be significant.

Dashes create a more dramatic break to the flow of a sentence than colons. They can add emphasis to a thought by making it visually prominent. The power of dashes can be understood by comparing the following sentences:

- I read every confusing word of my VCR instruction manual before tossing it into the trash.
- I read my VCR instruction manual—every confusing word—before tossing it into the trash.

Notice how the second sentence conveys a stronger
sense of frustration because of the way the phrase *every
confusing word* is isolated. The dashes effectively focus the
reader's attention on the key phrase.

Parentheses also can be appropriate for setting off a
thought—but it's usually an incidental thought. And as
you can see by comparing the following two sentences,
the effect is less than dramatic:

- Mary's shares of Coca-Cola, which her grandfather had bought decades ago, were worth a
  small fortune.
- Mary's shares of Coca-Cola (her grandfather
  had bought them decades ago) were worth a
  small fortune.

Notice that the second sentence is not significantly
different from the first. But it does give a little extra attention to the explanation about the origin of the shares
of stock.

Colons, dashes, and parentheses interrupt the continu-
ity of a sentence, thereby giving readers time to attend to

key words. So recovering malescribes should try to incorporate them judiciously into their sentences.

HEALING TIP:

Use colons, dashes, or parentheses when you want to focus the reader's attention momentarily.

Getting Things out of Order

"Did you hear about the guy who worried so much about punctuation that he developed digestive problems? He had an operation and ended up with a semicolon!"[6]

JOKES, OFTEN USED TO AVOID DEALING DIRECTLY with problems, can sometimes make valid points. In this case it is true that we shouldn't worry endlessly about punctuation and other structural aspects of our sentences. But healthy writing demands that we give them *adequate* attention—something that malescribes fail to do. So let's continue now with our look at structural mistakes in sentences.

Earlier in this chapter we learned about the principle of contiguity. Now let's turn our attention to another organizational principle: *sequence*.

When we read an account of a series of events or actions, we assume that they are presented in the correct temporal order. Why wouldn't they be? But if you've ever read any software user manuals (which typically are written by malescribes), you might have found your assumption to be unjustified. In fact, you might have come across instructions like the one below:

• Select "Save" from the "File" menu.

The problem with this instruction is that selecting "Save" is the *second* step in the process of saving a file, not the first (opening the "File" menu is the first). So it's up to the readers to act as editors. They must become aware of the sequence problem and then mentally transpose the sentence elements.

The previous unstructured example needs to be rewritten to reflect the correct order of events:

• Open the "File" menu and then select "Save."

Now the instruction has the elements in the order that common sense demands. The first step is presented first, and the second step is presented second. Any other arrangement doesn't make sense or serve any purpose.

Let's look at one more example of a sentence that has things in the wrong order:

- Remove the back panel of the amplifier, being careful first to unplug the device.

Since "remove the back panel" isn't the first step, why is it presented first? This unstructured sentence needs to be rewritten as follows:

- Unplug the amplifier first, and then remove the back panel.

Now the sentence is properly organized. No confusion is possible, and no rereading is necessary.

"First things first" is a principle that healthy writers follow instinctively. And they know that if they violate that principle, people will become confused and have to backtrack. So recovering malescribes should learn to be aware of sequence as they write.

HEALING TIP:

Present sentence elements in the sequence that makes the most sense.

Embracing Step 11

THE ELEVENTH STEP TOWARD RECOVERY WILL FREE you from the need to disregard commonsense organizational principles.

Step 11: Stop writing unstructured sentences.

In working through this step, you're deciding that you no longer will use your writing to rebel against your readers. By putting an end to unstructured writing, you're agreeing to give attention to punctuation, organization, and sequence of ideas. You're accepting the fact that a proper framework doesn't restrain expression but instead removes potential confusion about the way sentence elements are related.

To eliminate *unstructured sentences,* follow the healing tips given in this chapter:

- Never omit the final comma in a series.
- Keep the subject and verb of a sentence reasonably close together.
- Avoid splitting an infinitive unless doing so will create an awkward sentence.
- Help readers by grouping (and, if necessary, labeling) related items.

- Use colons, dashes, or parentheses when you want to focus the reader's attention momentarily.
- Present sentence elements in the sequence that makes the most sense.

Endnotes

1. A comma should appear after "colons."
2. Most of the verbiage between "My writing" and "isn't so bad" should be deleted or rewritten as another sentence.
3. "Boldly" separates two words that belong together ("to" and "state").
4. The sentence could be better organized: "My support system includes my pastor and therapist; my friends Ted and Jill; and my dogs Spot and Ralph."
5. The semicolon should be a colon.
6. There's no bad grammar here—just a bad joke.

STOP WRITING UNSIGHTLY SENTENCES

(by Overcoming Stubbornness)

NOT LONG AGO, THE PATH TO VERBAL ENLIGHTEN-ment would have had only eleven steps. Good writing was entirely a matter of putting clear, concise, convincing sentences onto paper—most likely with a typewriter. In steps 1 through 11, you've learned how to create effective sentences by eliminating many questionable writing techniques from your repertoire.

Today writing is more complex. Technology has placed sophisticated tools into our hands, and we are now confronted with many decisions about the *appearance* of our writing. Typewriters gave us few options about the way our sentences look on paper; personal computers have given us many. And on paper, as in life, first impressions are important. So a twelfth step is needed to take malescribes all the way to victory over their affliction.

In this step, we need to address the final obstacle on the road to recovery: *stubbornness*. Although malescribes don't refuse to use personal computers, they are reluctant to make the most of the new technological tools. They rigidly hold on to out-of-date habits and resist learning techniques that would make their writing more appealing to the eye. So let's learn about stubbornness and discover how it motivates malescribes to make bad decisions about the appearance of their text.

The Roots of Stubbornness

WE COULDN'T WRITE WHEN WE WERE TODDLERS, but we could express ourselves. And for most of us, the expression of choice was, "No!" Such defiance became routine during the most significant experience of those early years: potty training.

It was during this critical time that our parents optimistically expected us to begin learning to control ourselves. They wanted us to see the value of restraint. Instead, what we saw was a threat to our freedom and our sense of importance. So we deflected the threat by being *stubborn*. We refused to cooperate and continued to create the messes that we knew would have to be cleaned up by our increasingly impatient parents.

Stubbornness was an effective way—at least for a

while—to express defiance and also avoid accepting responsibility for our actions. We wanted to remain impulsive and unrestrained, and we expected others to tolerate the problems we created.

Although we eventually grew out of that difficult phase, it is unlikely that all of the emotional issues stirred up during that time were successfully resolved. Some of them simply got pushed "underground" so they could no longer influence us—or so we thought.

Today, many years later, your inner child-writer still feels the threat of those early traumatic encounters. It wants to resist and scream and refuse to cooperate. So the way adult malescribes subconsciously express this defiance is by making their writing visually uninviting. They carelessly create messy pages that are too dense, oddly formatted, or printed in small or unusual type. In other words, they write **unsightly sentences.**

Malescribes use a variety of techniques to make their sentences unsightly, and we'll examine them in this chapter. But first we need to have a brief vocabulary lesson.

Essential Terminology

PERSONAL COMPUTERS HAVE CHANGED NOT ONLY the way we *create* our writing, but also the way we *talk about* our writing. We now need to know a few basic words and phrases so we can better understand the choices we have concerning type and page layout. Here are some of the most important terms:

> *Typeface:* A unique design of letters, numbers, and special characters (for example, *Palatino*).
>
> *Font:* A typeface in a selected size and style (for example, twelve-point *Palatino* italic).
>
> *Point:* The unit used to measure type size (with seventy-two points equaling one inch). Most books and magazines use nine- to twelve-point type.
>
> *Body text:* Any relatively long block of text.
>
> *Display text:* Any relatively short block of text, such as a heading or advertising copy.
>
> *Leading (pronounced "ledding"):* The space between lines of text, measured in points.

These words and phrases—once jargon in the printing and publishing world—now should be part of every enlightened writer's vocabulary.

Let's look at some troubling errors malescribes make, resulting in a visual mess that tests the patience of their readers.

Making Text Lines Too Long

"I still set my margins at 1.25 inches, just like I did when I used a typewriter. That's okay, isn't it?"

THE TYPICAL TYPEWRITER FONT IS *MONOSPACED,* with each letter having the same width. But laser and ink-jet fonts are *proportionally spaced,* with letters having a variety of widths, from narrow *(i* and *l)* to wide *(m* and *w)*. Compare the following two versions of the same sentence set in the same type size (the first is set in *Courier,* and the second in *Berkeley Regular*). Notice the difference in the amount of space needed.

```
Time flies like an arrow.
```

Time flies like an arrow.

On a typewriter, setting left and right margins at 1.25 inches will yield an easy-on-the-eyes text line of 6 inches, or sixty characters (including spaces). But that same 6-inch text line written on a personal computer with a proportionally spaced font might contain *ninety characters or more*—unsightly and uninviting. If you've ever tried to read a lease or insurance policy, you know how repellent long lines of text are.

The 8.5 × 11-inch page is part of the problem. Ideally, the width of this standard paper size should have changed as we all began using proportionally spaced fonts. But because it didn't, we have to come up with solutions that limit the number of characters on a line. Here are a few possibilities:

- Widen the left and right margins.
- Use a slightly larger type size.
- Set the text in two columns.
- Use a proportionally spaced font with relatively wide letters. Compare the three sentences below:

> Once begun, the job's half-done.
> Once begun, the job's half-done.
> Once begun, the job's half-done.

The first sentence is set in *Times New Roman,* the second in *Century Book,* and the third in *Bookman.* You can see that the general shape of letters determines how much text can fit into a given horizontal space. The three typefaces don't differ in size (they are all set in 12-point type), only in the relative "fatness" of the letters. Fatter letters mean fewer characters per line.

What malescribes fail to realize is that space on a page

is not what's "left over." It is a graphic element, just as text and images are. Part of the recovery process is understanding that the visual appeal of *text* often depends on the creative use of *space*.

HEALING TIP:

Limit lines of body text to about sixty to seventy characters.

Degrading Text by Underlining It

WHEN WE USED TYPEWRITERS, UNDERLINING WAS the easiest way to add emphasis to a word or phrase. But underlining creates a visual problem, as you can see in the following sentence:

- Can you believe that Mrs. Greene was <u>jumping</u> on the furniture with her grandchildren?

Underlining cuts through the *descenders* (the parts of letters that extend downward), thereby making letters harder to recognize. If you use this technique, you are

making your sentence not only unsightly but more difficult to read as well.

A better way to add emphasis to text is to use italics.
Compare the following example with the previous one
and you'll appreciate the difference between underlined
and italic text:

• Can you believe that Mrs. Greene was *jumping* on
  the furniture with her grandchildren?

Italic type is distinctive and gets attention. But it's also
a bit harder to read than regular type, so use it sparingly.

Underlining is just another way malescribes create a
visual mess that they expect their readers to tolerate. It's
an out-of-date typewriter habit that has no place in the
world of laser and ink-jet printers.

HEALING TIP:

Use italics instead of underlining.

Using Inappropriate Leading

*"I like my computer because it makes a lot of the format-
ting decisions for me."*

YOUR WORD-PROCESSING PROGRAM ALLOWS YOU TO make decisions about the way your text is formatted. But if you don't, the program will use predetermined settings called *defaults*. Although most of us routinely override the default font and margins, we tend to be content with the default leading. But should we? Let's see how adjustments to the leading can sometimes have a positive effect on the visual appeal of text.

The default leading typically is equal to the type size plus about 20 percent. And this value usually produces visually pleasing results. But there are times when it's necessary to take matters into your own hands to avoid presenting unsightly sentences. Specifically, when you use either small or large type, you'll want to adjust the leading.

When you're using *small* type, it's important to *open* the leading—that is, to add a little more space between lines. (Sometimes, one additional point of leading can make a big difference.) Otherwise, your paragraphs will be uninviting gray masses. Compare the two paragraphs below:

Type provides a means of communicating verbal ideas visually. So does handwriting. But unlike handwritten characters, type is not spontaneous. Type has to be consciously selected and consciously arranged on a page. And type, although having a personality of its own, doesn't reflect the personality of the writer. An individual's handwriting may exist in only one style, but type comes in many hundreds of varieties.

Type provides a means of communicating verbal ideas visually. So does handwriting. But unlike handwritten characters, type is not spontaneous. Type has to be consciously selected and consciously arranged on a page. And type, although having a personality of its own, doesn't reflect the personality of the writer. An individual's handwriting may exist in only one style, but type comes in many hundreds of varieties.

Notice how the second paragraph is more inviting and easier to read because of the additional leading.

When you're using *large* type, as you would in a title or subheading, you'll want to *tighten* the leading (assuming that the text extends to two lines or more). In other words, you'll want to remove a little of the space between lines. Otherwise, the lines of text can appear unconnected. Compare the following two subheadings:

The Demands of Written Communication

The Demands of Written Communication

In the second version, you can see how the tighter leading holds the two lines together as a unit.

Although leading is not a feature of type, it does affect the way type looks. So recovering malescribes need to be willing to control leading when necessary to avoid creating unsightly sentences.

> **HEALING TIP:**
>
> Open leading for small type, but tighten leading for large type.

Using Serif and Sans Serif Fonts Interchangeably

"Sometimes text just seems hard to read. Why is that?"

THE LASER AND INK-JET FONTS THAT WE USE TODAY fall into four categories:

1. **Script:** Fonts that simulate handwriting. *New Berdina* is an example:

   Fourscore and seven years ago . . .

2. **Novelty:** Unconventional fonts that are designed to shock, amuse, or attract attention. *Hatmaker Regular* is an example:

FOURSCORE AND SEVEN YEARS
AGO . . .

3. **Serif:** Fonts with small strokes—serifs—extending from the main strokes of letters. *Century Schoolbook* is an example:

Fourscore and seven years
ago . . .

4. **Sans serif:** Fonts without serifs. *Futura* is an example:

Fourscore and seven years
ago . . .

Script and novelty fonts are usually reserved for relatively brief blocks of text in invitations, advertisements, and announcements. For most documents, we rely on serif and sans serif fonts.

You can see in the examples above that serif and sans serif fonts differ in appearance. But there's a more important difference: sentences are easier to read when set in a serif font. Why? First, serifs connect the letters of a word visually, helping to segregate the word from adjacent words. Second, serifs provide a horizontal element that guides the eyes. And finally, serif fonts are the ones we encounter most often.

So when you set your sentences in a serif font, you're cooperating with readers. You're presenting your ideas in a comfortable, familiar format.

Sans serif fonts can be appropriate for titles, subheadings, and other relatively small blocks of display text. But large blocks of sans serif type are unsightly and can be challenging to read.

HEALING TIP:

Use a serif font for the body of your documents.

Choosing Inappropriate Fonts

"The way I see it, a font is a font. The differences among fonts are minor, so it really doesn't matter which one I choose for my text."

WHEN USED PROPERLY, TYPE NOT ONLY CONVEYS A message, but also contributes to that message by suggesting a feeling. At the least, type should be unobtrusive—it shouldn't distract your readers. But type will be most effective when it's appropriate to the subject and consistent with the intent of the message.

Although it's true that any typeface can convey a message, typefaces vary considerably in the feelings they invoke. So a message might be enhanced by one typeface but weakened by another one. Compare the following two wedding invitations:

Mr. and Mrs. Reginald Finley
request the honor of your presence
at the marriage of their daughter,
Mary Lou, to Herman Krebbs,
on Saturday, May 9th,
at three in the afternoon.

Mr. and Mrs. Reginald Finley
request the honor of your presence
at the marriage of their daughter,
Mary Lou, to Herman Krebbs,
on Saturday, May 9th,
at three in the afternoon.

What's the difference? Both examples present the same message. The difference is that the first example suggests an elegant affair, while the second one doesn't. How can one font look so wrong and another one look so right?

Fonts differ only in physical features. But taken together, the combination of features gives a font a distinctive look that can be thought of as its character or personality. Formal or casual, traditional or contemporary, sturdy or delicate—these are just a few of the ways to characterize type.

Before people start to read a page, they see its general appearance and get an impression of what to expect. So when selecting a font for a document, be sure to think about the "between-the-lines" message you want to convey.

HEALING TIP:

Choose fonts that are consistent with the message of your document.

Using Odd Text Alignments

"I try to express my personality when I write, so sometimes I'll use creative formatting for paragraphs."

WORD-PROCESSING PROGRAMS ALLOW YOU TO ALIGN text on a page in four ways:

Flush left, with a ragged right edge:

The visual texture of a page is determined by
fonts, line and paragraph leading, margins,
text alignment, and other factors.

Flush right, with a ragged left edge:

The visual texture of a page is determined by
fonts, line and paragraph leading, margins,
text alignment, and other factors.

Centered, with ragged left and right edges:

The visual texture of a page is determined by
fonts, line and paragraph leading, margins,
text alignment, and other factors.

Justified, with straight left and right edges:

> The visual texture of a page is determined
> by fonts, line and paragraph leading,
> margins, text alignment, and other factors.

Research has shown that reading is facilitated when text lines have a consistent and predictable starting point. With flush left and justified text, this condition is met. Almost all books and magazines wisely follow this convention.

Healthy writers also follow the convention. They know that if they don't, they risk losing their readers' attention because reading will require too much effort.

But malescribes, seeing the writing process through their "stubbornness filter," resist accepting tried-and-true guidelines and instead rely on their own intuition. They will sometimes use centered and flush-right alignments for body text. They might defend their choice as being "creative." But in truth, they simply are creating unsightly sentences.

> **HEALING TIP:**
>
> Set text either flush left or justified, and reserve other alignments for occasional use with display text.

Embracing the Final Step

THE TWELFTH AND FINAL STEP WILL FREE YOU FROM the need to rely on outdated habits and uninformed decisions that make sentences visually unappealing.

Step 12: Stop writing unsightly sentences.

By working through this step, you're declaring that you no longer will guess at effective text formatting. In giving up unsightly sentences, you're conquering the self-destructive need for stubbornness. You're deciding that your emotions will not keep you from making healthy choices that will add to the visual appeal of your writing.

To eliminate unsightly sentences, keep this chapter's healing tips in mind:

- Limit lines of body text to about sixty to seventy characters.
- Use italics instead of underlining.
- Open leading for small type, but tighten leading for large type.
- Use a serif font for the body of your documents.
- Choose fonts that are consistent with the message of your document.
- Set text either flush left or justified, and reserve other alignments for occasional use with display text.

AFTERWORD

CONGRATULATIONS! YOU'VE WORKED THE TWELVE steps, and you're now "in recovery." Your efforts mean that you've made a commitment to healthy writing. You've beaten malescribism and loosened the shackles of questionable grammar and style. But as hard as it's been to achieve success, it might be even harder to maintain your healthy new habits.

Cured?

"I haven't split an infinitive, dangled a participle, or confused 'affect' with 'effect' for over a year. Doesn't that mean I'm cured, and can occasionally misplace a modifier without worrying?"

REMEMBER, THE SEEDS OF MALESCRIBISM ARE always present. Recovering doesn't mean you've flushed your emotional system of the disorder. At present, there is no known cure for malescribism. The best you can do is control it. Vigilance is needed to keep it from rising up and once again taking over your writing.

It's easy to slip back into old, counterproductive habits. So stay alert when you write, and remember the words that should have been written by the psychologist Emile Coué: "Every day, in every way, I am writing better and better!"

Recovering Malescribe's Bill of Rights

- I have the right to embrace Standard English.
- I have the right to respect my inner child-writer.
- I have the right to improve my writing skills without aiming for perfection.
- I have the right to create sentences without being motivated by negative emotions.
- I have the right to spell better than those around me.
- I have the right to be grammatically correct.
- I have the right to punctuate correctly without apology.
- I have the right to edit my work.
- I have the right to cooperate with my readers.
- I have the right to give myself permission to be a healthy writer.

INDEX

computers
  italic type for, 184
  leading and, 184–87
  margins on, 181–83
  terminology of, 179–80
  text alignments for, 192–94
  underlining and, 183–84
  use of spell checkers with, 117–18
  See also fonts
confidence in one's opinions, 47–48, 50*n6*
conjunctions, use of, 41, 149, 150
connotations, unintended, 115–17, 119*n5*
content, tone compared with, 122–23
contiguity, 163
continuous/continual, 109
contractions, avoidance of, 57–59, 67*n3*
control, overcoming need for, 6, 28
Coué, Emile, 198
creativity (originality)
  clichés instead of, 43–46, 50*n5*
  as excuse for bad writing, 11–12
  fear of, as showing off, 52

text alignment and, 193
criticism, malescribes' fear of, 34, 47–48, 50*n6*
cute, 94

dangling modifiers, 143–45, 156*n2*
dashes, use of, 170–71
deadwood, 82–83, 85*n6*
defaults, definition of, 185
defiance, overcoming need for, 6–7
demonstrative pronouns, ambiguous, 90–91
denial that one's writing is bad, 5, 9, 12, 17
denotations, definition of, 115
descenders, definition of, 183
discreet/discrete, 109
display text, definition of, 180
doubt, unpersuasive sentences and, 6, 120–38

each, verb with, 150
effect/affect, 108
either, verb with, 150–51
eminent/imminent, 109
encouraging agreement or action, 125–27, 138*n3*
ensure/insure, 110
etc., 91–93, 102*n2*

I, use of, 60
"if" statements, 63
imagery, persuasive, 129
imminent/eminent, 109
imply/infer, 110
imprecise terms, 134–35
in addition to, 150
incomplete comparisons, 96–97,
    102*n4*
incongruous sentences, 6,
    139–56
indifference
    to bad punctuation, 20
    unclear sentences and, 6,
       86–102
infer/imply, 110
infinitive phrases, dangling,
    145
infinitives, splitting, 165–67,
    176*n3*
information
    how to make readers
       remember, 128–30, 138*n4*
    omitting critical, 133–36,
       138*n6*
inner child-writer, 33–34, 53,
    69–70, 87, 104–5, 121,
    140–41, 159, 179
in other words, use of, 42
insecurity
    definition of, 34

weak sentences and. *See*
    sentences—weak
insure/ensure, 110
into/in, 110
italics, 184
    use of, 27, 31*n2*
its/it's, 117–18

jargon, 99–100, 102*n6*
justified text, 192–94

labels of groups, use of, 168–69
laborer, 116
laid/lay, 110
law firms, names of, as
    compound subjects, 149
lazy words, 93–96, 102*n3*
leading
    definition of, 180
    inappropriate, 184–87
less, in incomplete comparisons,
    97
less/fewer, 109
Living Well (typeface), 188
long sentences, 73–75, 85*n2*
lousy, 95

malescribism
    definition of, 9, 13–14
    See also bad writing
may/can, 108

Standard English
  nature of, 25
  suspicion of, 5, 24–29
stationery/stationary, 111
stone/rock, 115, 119*n5*
structure, need for, in writing,
  158, 167, 172
stubbornness
  roots of, 178–79
  unsightly sentences and, 7,
  177–95
subjects of sentences
  as essential sentence element,
  141
  separating verbs from,
  163–65, 176*n2*
  verb disagreement with,
  148–52, 156*n4*
subjunctive mood, 61–63, 67*n5*
super, 95
suspicion of Standard English,
  5, 24–29
syntax, abuse of, 11–12

terrible, 95
terrific, 116
text formatting, conventional
  and unconventional,
  19–20, 21
they, careless use of, 146–48,
  156*n3*

third person, referring to self in,
  56–57
this writer, 56–57
Times New Roman (typeface),
  182
tone, content compared with,
  122–23
too, 96–97, 102*n4*
transitional phrases, 42
typeface, definition of, 180
typewriters, 177, 181, 183

underlining, italics preferred to,
  27, 31*n2*, 183–84
unintended connotations,
  115–17, 119*n5*
unpersuasive sentences, 6,
  120–38
unsightly text, 7, 177–95
uppercase letters, 19, 23*n2*

vague references, 89–91, 102*n1*
verbs
  agreement between subjects
  and, 148–52, 156*n4*
  as essential elements of
  sentences, 141–43,
  156*n1*
  nonparallel, 112
  separating subjects from,
  163–65, 176*n2*

verbs *(continued)*
    tenses of, inconsistent use of,
       152–53, 156*n5*
very, 35
voice
    paralellism in, 112–13
    use and misuse of, 36–39,
       50*n2*

when?, 126
where?, 126
wishes, subjunctive mood and,
    61–63, 67*n5*
wordiness. *See* words—
    superfluous (redundant)
words
    clumsy, 15, 17*n3,* 57
    deadwood, 82–83, 85*n6*
    to encourage action, 126–27

"fancy," 28, 31*n4*
lazy, 93–96, 102*n3*
multisyllabic, 54
order of, 105–7, 119*n1*
pretentious, 54–56, 67*n1*
related, grouping of, 167–69,
    176*n4*
similar, confusion between,
    107–11, 199*n2*
sounds of, 114–15, 119*n4*
specialized, 99–100,
    102*n6*
superfluous (redundant), 15,
    17*n4,* 19, 21, 23*n1,*
    80–81, 85*n5*
vivid, 36, 52
wordy phrases, 70–72, 85*n1*
worry, shown by formal
    sentences, 5, 51–67

ABOUT THE AUTHOR

Robert W. Harris earned degrees in art as well as cognitive psychology and then made a living as a teacher for much of the 1980s. For the past fifteen years, he has worked as a freelance writer and instructional designer. In addition to writing eight books on personal computing and desktop publishing, he is also the author of *Fun with Phone Solicitors*. His Web site is rhauthor.com.